Introduction to Computer Science and Programming

HARPERCOLLINS COLLEGE OUTLINE

Introduction to Computer Science and Programming

Liia Vilms

HarperPerennial
A Division of HarperCollinsPublishers

Trademarks
IBM is a registered trademark of the International Business Machines Corporation.
Unix is a registered trademark of Bell Laboratories.
Microsoft and **MS-DOS** are registered trademarks of Microsoft Corporation.
Ada is a registered trademark of the U.S. Government.
All other brand and product names are trademarks or registered trademarks of their
respective companies.

Developed by American BookWorks Corporation
Project Manager: Mary Mooney
Editor: Margaret Tuttle

Library of Congress Cataloging-in-Publication Data

Vilms, Liia, 1937–
    Introduction to computer science and programming / Liia Vilms.
        p.   cm.
    Includes bibliographical references and index.
    ISBN 0-06-467145-3
    1. Computer science. 2. Pascal (Computer program language)
I. Title.
QA76.V515 1993   91-58277
ISBN 0–06–467145–3—dc20

94 95 96 97 98 ABW/RRD 10 9 8 7 6 5 4 3 2 1

Contents

Preface

A variety of approaches are used in introductory computer science courses, whether taught at the college level or in earlier high school AP classes. A course may focus on problem solving and algorithm development or on the specifics of a particular programming language, and may also include more general topics in software development or hardware architectures. The goal of this book is to outline major topics and provide supplementary material to the textbook chosen for an introductory computer science course, whatever the primary orientation of the course.

The material in the book is divided into two parts. Part I covers general concepts of computer science and Part II describes the details of programming in a high-level language. Pascal has been chosen as the representative language because of its wide use as an introductory language in programming courses, as well as its popularity for software development in general. The focus in the Pascal section of the book is on those statements which are representative of programming techniques in other procedural languages and are typically covered in an introductory course. More advanced features, such as Pascal's extensive data definition capabilities, are beyond the scope of this book. The topic coverage of Part I can also serve as an overview of important concepts in computer science for students in other disciplines who need an understanding of such background material.

The choice of topics for the book has been influenced by "A Report of the ACM Curriculum Committee Task Force for CS1" (Communications of the Association for Computing Machinery, October 1984) and the May 1991 computer science course guidelines for the Advanced Placement program of the Educational Testing Service. A bibliography of suggested readings is provided after Appendix A.

The chronological overview of the major stages of computer hardware and software development presented in Chapter 1 has been particularly interesting to write because I have experienced these developments personally during my career as a computer scientist. As a college student, I had the opportunity in 1959 to manage the operations of a multi-million dollar vacuum tube–based IBM 709 computer, and a few years later to participate in the exploration of compiler and operating system techniques at IBM for the next generation of transistor-based machines. In the 1970s my students in programming classes at Colorado State University were debugging their FORTRAN programs on mainframes and were being introduced to interactive computing via remote terminals. In the 1980s my software development work was done on the minicomputers and increasingly powerful engineering workstations of my high-tech employer, the Hewlett-Packard Co. The completion of this book in 1993 on a portable "laptop" computer was another opportunity to take advantage of the latest computer technology.

I am especially grateful for the help and advice provided by my friend, Professor Paul DuChateau, for writing this book. My husband, Jaak, and my mother, Antonia Annus, have been wonderfully supportive, and the encouragement of my sons Andres and Thomas has made the effort worthwhile. I wish to express my thanks as well to Ms. Mary Mooney and Ms. Margaret Tuttle for their valuable editorial assistance and to Mr. Fred N. Grayson of American BookWorks Corporation for his guidance. Finally, I thank HarperCollins Publishers for the opportunity to contribute as an author to their College Outline Series.

Liia Vilms
Ft. Collins, Colorado

PART I—COMPUTER HARDWARE AND SOFTWARE

1

The Development of Modern Computer Systems

*The techniques implemented in modern computer systems have evolved from a desire to automate the basic steps of counting and arithmetic, largely in order to eliminate human error. The use of an early counting device, the **abacus**, has been traced back to the civilizations of China, Greece, and Rome. Beads on rods represent groups of numbers on an abacus, and the human user provides the input, output, and processing power by manipulating the beads and recognizing results from their arrangements.*

The invention of mechanical computational devices from the mid-17th to the late-18th centuries was the beginning of computer history. These devices, which represented information digitally and used a series of instructions to automatically control a loom or a set of gears, embodied the concepts that are basic to automatic computation.

With the addition of electricity and ever faster technological developments since the 1940s, computers today have achieved fantastic computational power and a wide range of applications beyond numeric computation.

EARLY MECHANICAL DEVICES

Mathematicians and physical scientists of the 17th and 18th centuries relied on printed numerical tables of computations such as multiplication, logarithms, trigonometric functions, etc., to aid them in their work. Early scientists had great interest in creating such tables automatically because manual creation of the tables was tedious, and the large books of tables were often full of errors.

Blaise Pascal (1623–1662)

The mathematician and philosopher, Blaise Pascal, developed a mechanical counting device in 1642 when he was just nineteen. His small device was capable of performing both addition and subtraction on numbers which were set on a dial with a pointed stylus.

The programming language **Pascal** has been named for this early pioneer in automatic computing.

Gottfried Wilhelm Leibniz (1646–1716)

Leibniz, another mathematician and philosopher, developed a mechanism based on a number wheel which allowed his device to do automatic multiplication and division, as well as addition and subtraction operations.

Charles Babbage (1791–1871)

Computer history is often traced back to Babbage, because his ideas included the use of a **program** to control his mechanical computing devices. Babbage borrowed the idea of using **punched cards** to control the operation of his machines from looms developed by **Joseph Jacquard** in France. Jacquard looms used holes in punched cards to control the patterns which were woven by the threads. These looms were immediately successful when introduced in the early 1800s.

DIFFERENCE ENGINE

Babbage's first attempt to build a mechanical device to do automatic computation was a **Difference Engine**. The machine consisted of numerous interlocking gear wheels whose positions represented decimal numbers. It was based on the mathematical theory of polynomials and was meant to perform additions in a specific sequence to produce its results. Although a portion of "Difference Engine No.1" was successfully completed in 1832, Babbage never built the complete device. However, Georg and Edvard Scheutz, a Swedish father and son team who were inspired by Babbage's work, successfully built a working difference engine in 1843.

ANALYTICAL ENGINE

Babbage also conceived a more general-purpose computational device which he called the **Analytical Engine** and worked on designs for this machine from 1834 until his death. Although only portions of it were ever built, its design included concepts that are basic to modern computer design. The engine was to be directed by punched cards, and included a "store" where numbers and results would be held, and a "mill" to perform the calculations. The engine's design also included "branching" and "looping" operations which are common in modern programming languages.

The reasons for Babbage's lack of success in completing his revolutionary machines have been a matter of historical debate. In honor of the bicentenary of Babbage's birth, his designs for "Difference Engine No.2" were used to successfully build this device at the Science Museum of London. It is on display at the museum with other interesting materials from Babbage's pioneering work in computer design.

Ada Lovelace
(1816–1852)

Augusta Ada Byron, the daughter of Lord Byron the poet, and later the Countess of Lovelace, was a mathematician who worked with Charles Babbage on his designs and reported on his work. In recognition for her early work as a programmer, the programming language **Ada** has been named for her.

ELECTROMECHANICAL DEVICES

Electrically controlled tabulators, developed by Herman Hollerith in the 1890s, are regarded as an important foundation for modern computer development. More complex computing devices combining mechanical relay switches with electronic components followed, and led to the development of the first completely electronic digital computers in the 1940s.

Herman
Hollerith
(1860–1929)

Herman Hollerith won a competition to speed up the tabulation of results from the 1890 census by designing an electrically powered tabulator. His tabulators and sorters dramatically reduced the time to produce census results from the seven and a half years it had taken in the 1880s. The new punched card technology proved to be commercially successful, and the Tabulating Machine Company which Hollerith founded later became the International Business Machines Company (IBM) in 1924.

The data representation scheme developed for punched cards (known as **Hollerith code**) was basic to the design of early computers and languages. Punched card devices were still widely used to prepare computer input in the 1960s and early 1970s.

Mark I

Howard Aiken of Harvard University pursued Babbage's earlier ideas to design a machine suitable for scientific computations. The result of his joint work with IBM was the **Automatic Sequence Controlled Calculator**, known as the **Mark I**, which was completed in 1944. The calculator contained electrically controlled relays and counters for storing decimal numbers. It also had 60 registers into which numbers could be manually entered by switch settings.

ENIAC

The **Electronic Numerical Integrator and Calculator** was developed at the Moore School of Engineering at the University of Pennsylvania and became operational in 1946. It was designed to calculate ballistic data for the military and included large banks of electro-mechanical switches in addition to electronic circuitry. Just as the Mark I, the **ENIAC** was large and complex, and required teams of people to enter numbers by manually setting its 6000 switches.

The computations of both the Mark I and the **ENIAC** were controlled by instructions read from punched cards. The **ENIAC** incorporated vacuum tubes in its electronic circuitry and was able to perform calculations much faster than the earlier Mark I which used far slower electro-mechanical relays.

EARLY ELECTRONIC COMPUTERS

EDVAC

The **Electronic Discrete Variable Calculator** was also developed at the Moore School and incorporated more sophisticated ideas which evolved from the ENIAC's design. It is regarded as the first general purpose electronic computer because its design was based on the fundamental ideas of a general instruction set and a **stored program**. Vacuum tubes were utilized for the circuitry, and both numbers and program instructions were stored electronically in the computer's memory.

John von Neumann (1903–1957)

The mathematician John von Neumann worked with the scientists at the Moore School to develop new concepts of automatic computation, first incorporated into the design of the **EDVAC**. He was the principal author of an influential paper describing the logical organization of a general purpose computational machine. His work at Princeton's Institute for Advanced Study in the late 1940s refined earlier ideas into the fundamental concepts of computer architecture which are known today as the "von Neumann machine." This architecture is basic to modern computer design, and includes the ideas of binary number computation, memory for data storage, input and output devices, and overall logical control by means of instructions stored in memory and decoded serially.

UNIVAC

The **Universal Automatic Computer** was the first commercially built computer and also evolved from the work done at the Moore School. It was intended for business applications as well as scientific computations, and was delivered to the U.S. Census Bureau in 1951 to tabulate the results of the previous year's census.

MAINFRAMES

After the basic concepts of computer design evolved from university research of the 1940s, IBM, Sperry-Rand, and other companies began to build and sell computers for commercial use.

The early computers were large enough to fill a room, and were intended to do complex numerical calculations and tabulations at speeds far greater than humans could possibly achieve. These computers became known as **mainframes**, and the term is still used today to describe the largest and fastest of our modern computers.

First Generation— 1950s

Technological advances which took place in the three decades from the early 1950s to the late 1970s had a profound impact on computer design. Because the design of computers was fundamentally affected by each major change in technology, the development of modern computers is often described in terms of the "generations" in which a particular technology was used. The overall design of a computer's electronic circuitry and its logical functionality is usually called its **architecture**.

ARCHITECTURE

The first commercial mainframe computers utilized **vacuum tubes**, similar to those used in early radios, for their electronic circuitry. Because of the heat generated by the tubes, the machines were subject to frequent breakdowns and had to be operated in air-conditioned surroundings.

The memory in these early computers consisted of thousands of **magnetic cores**. Information was stored in **memory cells**, each of which was composed of a set of tiny cores, shaped like rings, which were magnetized to represent either an "on" or "off" state. The term **core** is still sometimes used to refer to a computer's memory.

STORED PROGRAM

The series of instructions which controlled the computer's operations was known as a **program**, and was written in a coded form known as

machine language. It was the responsibility of the **programmer** who wrote the instructions to know the codes representing the computer's instruction set, and to keep track of all numbers and memory cells used in the computations.

The first computers typically processed a single program at a time, after a human operator had set the necessary external switches and readied the input and output devices.

PERIPHERAL DEVICES

Punched cards were the primary **input** and **output** media for the early mainframe computers. Devices which processed the cards, such as card readers, keypunches, sorters, etc., became known as **peripheral devices**.

In addition to punched card input and output, **magnetic tapes** came into use as a medium for data storage. Input and output to tapes was faster than punched cards, and tapes were easier to handle manually than large trays of cards. Data was often transferred from cards to tapes by a **peripheral** computer, which was smaller and slower than the mainframe.

Second and Third Generations— 1960s

ARCHITECTURE

Second generation. Computer design was transformed by the invention of **transistors**, providing very fast electronic switches that required far less power than vacuum tubes. Electronic circuitry based on transistors became the foundation of computer architecture in the early 1960s. Smaller, faster, and more reliable machines could now be built, which no longer required the cooling of earlier machines. IBM took advantage of the new technology with its **Series 360** architecture, and built a family of computers with varying power and memory capacity.

Third generation. The technological advance of **integrated circuits** in the late 1960s again revolutionized computer design. Transistors and other electronic circuits were etched onto tiny pieces of silicon crystal to form **integrated circuits** (ICs). These silicon **chips** may be just an eighth of an inch square and yet contain most of the computing power of a computer. The miniaturized circuitry on chips provided still greater speed and reliability and allowed even smaller devices to be built at lower cost.

SYMBOLIC LANGUAGES

Together with the advances in technology which led to more sophisticated computer design, programming languages also evolved during the 1960s. At first, symbolic representations were defined for computer instructions because **machine language** programming of early computers was very tedious and prone to error. The next improvement was the development of **higher-level languages** which allowed program instructions to be expressed in a form much closer to human language.

Assembly language. Easily remembered codes were assigned to a computer's instruction set, and memory cells and steps within the program itself could be identified by symbols. For example, the code MPY might represent the multiplication instruction, and the symbol DATE could be the name of a memory cell in which a date was stored.

FORTRAN. The **FORmula TRANslation** language was defined in the late 1950s as one of the first high-level languages. The language allowed a programmer to express instructions for numerical calculations in a format very similar to algebraic equations. Symbolic names could be used to manipulate data values, and special input and output statements controlled the data read from cards or sent to a printer.

COBOL. The **COmmon Business-Oriented Language** was an English-like language introduced in 1959 to describe computations more typical of business applications. It also allowed symbolic expression of computations and provided control for handling large volumes of data.

LISP. The **LISt Processing** language was developed at MIT in the late 1950s to allow high-level processing of symbols. The language was primarily used at universities until it found new popularity in the 1980s for **artificial intelligence** programming.

TRANSLATORS

Since each computer can only process instructions given in its own machine language, programs written in higher-level languages must be translated to machine-understandable form. Techniques of translation were developed together with the new languages of the 1960s.

Assemblers were developed to convert program instructions from assembly languages into the machine language which could be decoded by a computer's processor. **Compilers** were written to translate program statements from FORTRAN and COBOL to machine language, which would then be transferred by a program called a **loader** into the computer's memory for processing. Some languages, such as LISP, did not go through a first-pass compilation step, but were processed by an **interpreter** which translated and executed each program statement dynamically.

OPERATING SYSTEM

As the speed of computers increased, and high-level languages led to more complex programming tasks, there was a need to automate the various scheduling and coordinating activities still performed by the human computer operator. A program known as an **operating system** was designed for each computer, to control the overall processing of the machine. It was the function of this program to schedule and monitor the stages of each **job**, and to manage the transfer of data between input and output devices.

Batch processing. In order to optimize the computer's performance, jobs that were similar in their requirements were grouped together into **batches** and run sequentially. For instance, if several FORTRAN programs were to be compiled, they would be run one after the other. In this way the handling of tapes needed by the compiler could be minimized.

Job Control Language. In order to minimize operator intervention, a language called **JCL** was developed to give instructions to IBM's OS360 operating system. JCL cards were inserted between the card decks of each job to direct the operating system as to how each job was to be processed. A whole series of jobs could be run at night, for instance, with very little intervention by an operator.

MASS STORAGE

Magnetic tapes remained the primary large-capacity storage media for the early mainframe computers until the development of **disk drives** in the mid-1960s. Once disks came into use, they provided permanent storage and fast access to large quantities of data. The operating system, user programs, and data were all stored on disks, and the immediate access to the data eliminated the time lost in manual mounting and unmounting of tapes.

TIME SHARING

Although the processing power of computers was increasing with technological advances, the speed of input and output operations was not keeping pace. As a result, **time sharing** techniques were developed to control computer operations in such a way that input and output activity (generally known as **I/O**) would not slow down the primary computations. Also, because computers were large and expensive, it was economically advantageous to allow access to their processing power to more than a single user at a time.

Multiprocessing

Operating system techniques were developed in the mid-1960s which allowed the operations of a program to be broken down into tasks, each needing a different resource of the computer. Each task, or **process**, was allowed a brief interval of time for execution before control was passed to another task. This idea of time sharing allowed computing operations to be interspersed with the slower and intermittent operations of the input and output devices.

Interactive Computing

In the early 1970s, existing **teletypes** and **VDTs** (Video Display Terminals) with keyboards came into use as I/O devices for mainframe computers. Instead of an operator submitting jobs to a computer via punched cards or magnetic tape, users could sit at a remote **terminal** and communicate directly with the computer. Time sharing allowed many users to be communicating with a computer at the same time. Although each user was sharing the computer's power with others, the relative speed of the computer processor to human reaction and response time allowed users to perceive that they had sole control of the computer.

For instance, the new interactive techniques allowed students working on programming assignments for a computer class to develop their programs **on-line**, rather than carry around card decks which were handed in for a computer run at the university's computer center. Student programs were stored on the university mainframe's disk, and each student could work on his program while sitting at a terminal which was directly connected to the computer.

MICROCOMPUTERS

Fourth Generation— 1970s

Further technological advances in the 1970s led to **Very Large Scale Integration** of chip circuitry and produced ever-smaller chips containing thousands of circuits. These **VLSI** chips were known as **microprocessors** and could contain all of a computer's logic circuits on a single chip. It was the task of the microprocessor to decode the computer's instructions, known as **microcode**, and to activate the circuits needed by each operation.

The VLSI technology has been fundamental to the development of modern computer power and the evolution of **personal computers** in the 1980s.

Minicomputers

Smaller computers known as **minicomputers** were developed in the 1970s to make computing power more accessible. Although these computers had the same essential functionality as mainframes, they were designed to be produced at lower cost. Their primary difference was an architecture based on a shorter computer word of **16-bits**, versus the **32-bits** in use for larger computers. The shorter computer word implied smaller memory capacity, and somewhat slower speed. (The organization of computers and the binary representation of data in computer memory are described in Chapters 2 and 3.)

Because the technology no longer required cooling, the computers were often in people's work areas, rather than remote computer rooms. Most minicomputers were powerful enough to be **multiuser** systems, supporting interactive use from a number of **terminals**.

Personal
Computers

The continued miniaturization of electronic devices led to the eventual development of low-cost computers intended for personal use. The first example of this phenomenon was the **MITS Altair**, introduced in 1975. It was intended for computer aficionados, and included switches and dials to be manipulated by the user, just like the very early mainframes. The **Apple** computer and others introduced in the late 1970s proved to be more convenient. They included a keyboard for input and a display screen for output, and provided data storage on small cartridge tapes, or disk drives which processed removable **floppy disks**. With the introduction of the **IBM PC** in 1981, businesses began to use such **personal computers** to complement their mainframes, and to introduce computing to areas where it had never been used before.

DOS

Although Apple computers relied on their own proprietary operating system, most other PCs in the 1980s adopted the **Disk Operating System** developed by Microsoft for the IBM PC. DOS provides the basic functions for a **single user** to handle data storage and to control input and output devices and program execution.

GRAPHICAL USER INTERFACE

With the introduction of the **Macintosh** computer by Apple in 1984, new ways of interaction with a computer were introduced.

Information was presented to the user via pictures, known as **icons**, on the computer's display screen, and a new hand-held input device, called a **mouse**, was available for selecting choices from the screen. The "Mac" utilized a **bit-mapped display** which is able to display both graphics and text. Each graphical image is composed of small dots called **pixels** which must be manipulated individually by the computer's programs.

PC SOFTWARE

The popularity of PCs grew rapidly in the 1980s as innovative **application programs** were developed to enable nontechnical users to do useful tasks on the computer. **Word processors** allow a user to write and edit text, **spreadsheet programs** provide convenient computational power for data stored in tables, and **business graphics** programs are able to display data in the form of graphs and charts.

The programs needed to direct a computer's operations and solve problems are known collectively as **software.** The term **hardware** describes the physical devices that form the computer itself.

Workstations

As the computing power of microprocessor chips increased, it became possible to run complex numbercrunching scientific and engineering programs on small, powerful computers known as **engineering workstations**. Although many of these computers are not much larger than PCs and are meant mainly for a single user, these **multiprocessing** systems are designed to handle multiple tasks in the same time shared manner as larger mainframes. They are thus well suited for networking use (see below).

In the late 1980s a new form of VLSI computer architecture called **RISC**, or **Reduced Instruction Set Computing**, was introduced to eliminate the complexity of earlier **CISC**, or **Complex Instruction Set Computing** microcode. The simplified instruction sets allow the new RISC processor chips to compute at speeds measured in the millions of instructions per second (MIPS).

NETWORKED COMPUTING

The widespread use of computing has brought with it the desire for users to access computers which are at a distance, and to share data and transmit messages between computers. The evolution and development of **computer networks** in the 1980s has enabled data and computing power to be shared in many innovative ways. Modern airline reservation systems, for instance, would not be possible without the ability to transmit and share information over distances at great speed.

Telephone Lines

An electronic device called a **modem** allows computers to transmit data over telephone lines. A modem at the sending side converts the electronic digital data into signals suitable for sending over a telephone line. The signals are decoded and converted to digital computer data again by a modem at the receiving end.

Thus a computer user who has a PC with a modem at home can dial a call to the modem of an office computer and transmit data between the PC and the office machine.

LAN

A **Local Area Network** allows computers in reasonable proximity of each other to be connected by cabling over which data can be transmitted from one machine to another without the use of commercial phone lines. Such **networking** allows users to share data, and also use common peripheral devices. The costs of a plotter, or an expensive laser printer, can be shared for instance, by connecting the peripheral to the network, and allowing all network users to send their output data to the device.

Distributed Computing

The communication between computers that are linked together in a network may occur over the LAN cables which connect a set of office PCs in a building, or over telecommunication lines which can reach computers in different parts of the world.

The increased popularity of computer networks provides an opportunity to divide complex computing tasks among computers with varying processing power. Mainframes can store large amounts of data or do heavy-duty computations, for instance, while cheaper and slower computers in the network can interact with users and handle tasks which do not require as much processing power.

For example, a company may keep all its engineering drawings on a central computer with large storage capacity at its headquarters, while engineers at branch offices can **download** any drawing to a local computer for modification. Similarly, a user may submit a request to run a statistical program on a university computer, where a special control program analyzes the workload on all computers in the network and assigns the job to an available computer with adequate processing capability. The user will get the results, and may not even know that the calculations were done in a different state on another university's mainframe.

Such techniques of shared processing over networks are generally called **distributed computing**. A computer that provides the core of the services is called a **server**, while any computer requesting a service is known as a **client**.

Although the ideas of automatic computation were explored more than 200 years ago in an effort to produce reliable results from mathematical calculations, the history of modern computers truly began about 50 years ago. The university research done in the 1940s defined the fundamental principles of computer architecture and the extraordinary technological advances of the 1970s spurred the development of computers which are so fast, reliable, and affordable that they are in use all over the world.

Advances in software techniques have accompanied each stage of hardware development and computing power is available today in many variations. Computer chips are embedded in video games and ballistic missiles. Computer programs analyze election returns, maintain supermarket inventories, and draw images of the brain on a display screen. Networks of computers make immediate reservations for a vacation trip possible, and help analyze worldwide weather patterns.

The basic functionality of computer systems which makes such a range of applications possible is described in the following chapters.

2

Computer Organization

*A*ll *modern computers, whatever their size or speed, share the same essential functionality. Computers must be able to accept information as input, perform computations on data, and produce output in a form understandable by humans. Today's computers provide data storage in speedily accessible internal memory, or on devices like CD-ROMs or optical disks which are slower, but have the advantage of permanence and large capacity. An integral part of modern computer design is also an internally stored program directing the overall flow of processing.*

To perform its essential operations, the electronic circuitry of a computer is organized into five major functional areas. (1) **Main memory** *contains the programs and data which must be directly accessible for the computer's operation. The (2)* **CPU** *(central processing unit) directs the overall flow of the computer's processing and performs arithmetic and logical operations. (3)* **Input** *devices accept data from the outside and translate the information into computer-understandable form. (4)* **Output** *devices direct the results of the computer's processing to humans, via appropriate devices such as printers or a video screen, and (5)* **auxiliary memory** *devices allow large quantities of data to be stored on a permanent basis.*

DATA REPRESENTATION

The information which a computer processes is generally known as **data**. Individual **data values** may represent numbers, alphabetic characters, or other coded information. The computer programs which direct the computer's operations are also data, because the instructions which they contain must be stored in the computer's memory before they are able to be processed.

All information in modern computers is stored and processed in **binary** form, that is, as a series of 0s and 1s. The evolution of modern computer architecture which was described in Chapter 1 has proved that electronic circuits can be efficiently designed to represent a two-state information system. Electronic signals can rapidly switch between "off" and "on" states, and these states can easily represent the binary digits zero and one. Each binary digit, commonly called a **bit**, represents the smallest unit of information which can be stored in the computer.

Bits are grouped into longer units known as **bytes** to hold more meaningful data. Each **byte** is eight bits in length and may represent a numeric value, an alphabetic character, or other coded information.

Most computers use a standard coding system for representing a byte of data as an alphabetic character. The two most common coding systems, ASCII and EBCDIC, are described in Appendix A.

Since all information is stored in the computer's memory, the length of a binary data value which can be stored in each memory **cell** (defined below) is determined by the computer's design.

A computer **word** defines the number of bits which can be stored in a memory cell. Minicomputers typically have memory words of 16 bits (two bytes), while computers with complex functionality have been designed with word lengths as long as 64 bits. A longer computer word can represent larger numeric values and can store more bytes of character data. It can also access a larger memory because there is room to hold bigger memory addresses in the computer's instructions.

The example below illustrates various patterns of binary information (also called **bit strings**) which may be stored in a computer's memory. Common information coding schemes and the rules of binary arithmetic are more completely described in Chapter 3.

EXAMPLE 1.

(a) The 16-bit memory cell of a minicomputer might contain the following bits.

```
0100000101011010
   A        Z
```

According to the ASCII character code (defined in Appendix A), the two bytes can be interpreted as the characters "AZ".

(b) A 32-bit computer word which contains the bit string:

```
00000000000000000000011001010001
```
represents the positive number 1617.

(c) A 36-bit computer word which contains the binary instruction:

111001000000000000000000000010011011
op code   address

means "add the data in memory cell 155" if the code 111001 represents an "ADD" instruction for this computer.

DATA STORAGE

Main Memory

Main memory is that part of a computer's electronic circuitry which holds the binary data which the computer's program will process.

PHYSICAL ORGANIZATION

Address. Memory is divided into individual **cells**, also known as **storage locations**, (or **core** memory, an older term described in Chapter 1). Each memory cell is assigned a specific **address**, from 0 to the maximum size of the computer's memory capacity. If a particular computer has 32,767 memory locations (abbreviated to 32K as described below), there will be individual memory cells with addresses which range from 0 to 32766.

When any computer program instruction needs to retrieve a data value from memory, it must specify the address at which the value is stored.

EXAMPLE 2.

Memory cells are often compared to mailboxes. If a customer has rented a mailbox at his branch Post Office, he must specify the number of his post office box to the friends who will write to him, and can only retrieve his letters from the box assigned to him.

Similarly, a computer may have salary information stored in memory cells with addresses from 1200 to 1500. A program which prints paychecks for employees can retrieve the information by addressing these memory locations when processing the salary information.

Size. The size of a computer's memory is stated in terms of how many addressable memory locations it contains. Because the binary number system is fundamental to the design of computers, the size is typically specified in terms of a number which is a power of 2. The letter **K** (which stands for **kilobyte**) is used as a shorthand notation for 1000, but in computer terms it is actually 2^8, i.e., 1024. (Binary representation of numbers is defined in Chapter 3.)

EXAMPLE 3.

(a) A personal computer which is advertised to have 256K bytes of memory will have approximately 256,000 memory cells, each capable of storing a byte of data. The exact number is

$$256 \times 1024 = 262,144 \text{ bytes.}$$

(b) An engineering workstation is sold with 16M bytes of storage. The letter **M** is common shorthand notation for a **megabyte** or million bytes, which is actually $2^{20} = 1,048,576$. So, the workstation is able to store over 16 million bytes of information, or 16,777,216 bytes to be exact.

Hardware. With current VLSI technology, the electronic circuits representing memory are etched on chips known as **RAM** chips. Arrays of RAM chips are arranged on printed circuit **memory boards** which are installed inside the main computer unit. RAM chips may also be arranged on small SIMM memory boards which are connected directly to the computer's system board. It is possible to expand the memory capacity of most computers simply by adding additional RAM boards.

ATTRIBUTES

Random access. Main memory is known as "random access memory" (hence the name RAM), because all memory locations are equally accessible at the same speed, no matter how the memory cells are physically arranged in the computer.

High-speed. Main memory is so designed that the computer's instructions can access data directly from the cells at high speeds. Access to information stored on auxiliary memory devices is much slower however, because it must first be transferred to main memory before it is accessible to program instructions.

Read/Write capability. Computer instructions can write (store) information into a cell in main memory, or read (retrieve) information from a cell. When information is stored, the previous information in the cell is destroyed. When information is read, it is merely copied, and the original value remains in the cell until a new value is stored there.

Volatility. The main memory of the computer will contain data only when power to the computer is turned on. All information will be lost from main memory when the computer's power is turned off, and must be restored before processing can continue.

ROM Memory

ROM, or "read-only" memory, is a specialized part of main memory which is designed to prevent data loss when the power to the computer is turned off. ROM memory circuits are also stored on chips which are directly accessible by the computer's instructions. However, ROM memory has the following unique features.

CHARACTERISTICS

Read-only. The information stored in ROM can only be read, and new information cannot be stored into the ROM memory cells.

Permanence. Information which is stored into ROM locations is **non-volatile** and will not disappear when power to the computer is turned off.

Typical use. Because of its special characteristics, ROM memory is reserved for critical program instructions which must be immediately available when a computer is first turned on.

For example, the instructions which are the very first to execute, or **boot** a system, when power is turned on, are typically stored in ROM. The machine instructions are programmed into ROM chips by special processes at the factory, and cannot be later changed without physically replacing the chips.

CENTRAL PROCESSING UNIT

At the heart of each computer is its **CPU**, whose electronic circuitry performs two major functions. The **Control Unit** has the overall task of controlling and coordinating the computer's operations, while the **Arithmetic/Logical Unit** (also known as the **ALU**), performs all arithmetic computations and logical operations.

Control Unit

PROGRAM EXECUTION

All the operations of a computer are directed by a set of instructions, known as a **program**, which is stored in the computer's main memory. The control unit locates the appropriate instructions, controls their sequencing, and executes them by activating appropriate circuitry.

Instructions. Each computer has a unique **instruction set** determined by the designers of its architecture. Each instruction includes a code that specifies the operation to be performed, and the memory address of the data value to be acted on.

Although specific instruction formats may differ, all computers have instructions to perform arithmetic, to move data within the computer's memory, and to test data for program decisions. Instructions also exist to transfer data between various input and output devices and memory.

Sequence. The control unit processes instructions sequentially, that is, in the order in which they are found in successive memory locations. Transfer to a new memory location occurs only when a specific transfer instruction is executed.

Program Counter. The program counter is a special-purpose memory location which always contains the memory address of the instruction that is currently being processed (executed). A **transfer of control** is said to occur when the address in the program counter changes, and the control unit executes the instruction at the new address.

Instruction Counter. The instruction counter is another special-purpose memory cell which contains the instruction currently being processed. The control unit executes the instruction by decoding the operation code of the instruction and activating all necessary circuits to complete the operation.

HARDWARE CHARACTERISTICS

CPU chip. The circuitry of the CPU is contained on one or more **chips**. As was described in Chapter 1, chips are tiny electronic devices made of silicon, which contain thousands of integrated circuits.

Clock/cycle time. The CPU of a computer synchronizes its operations by the regular pulses emitted by an electronic device called a **clock**. Most instructions are executed during one pulse of the clock; the basic execution time of an instruction is known as **cycle time**.

Speed. The speed of a computer may be quoted in a number of ways. Sometimes, speed is specified as **clock speed**, such as 33 MHz (MegaHertz, or million cycles per second). Speed may also be quoted as the number of instructions the CPU can execute in a second (**MIPS**, a million instructions a second), or the unit of time it takes to execute one instruction.

Units of time common in computer speed quotations are the following.
millisecond—one thousandth of a second : 1/1000,
microsecond—one millionth of a second : 1/1,000,000, and
nanosecond—one billionth of a second : 1/1,000,000,000.

Arithmetic / Logical Unit

COMPUTATIONS

All computations done by the **ALU** are performed on binary values, and follow the rules of binary arithmetic. (A discussion of binary data representation and binary arithmetic and logic follows in Chapter 3.)

Although the ALU performs only very basic arithmetic operations, complex computations can be done at great speed by combining and repeating the basic operations.

Arithmetic operations. The arithmetic unit performs the basic operations for addition, subtraction, multiplication and division. Instructions exist for arithmetic on integer values, as well as computations on numbers with fractions (known in computer science as **real** numbers).

Registers. The ALU contains special memory cells, known as **registers**, in which the arithmetic is carried out. Data values must first be moved from main memory to a register, for arithmetic to be performed, and the result must be moved again to a memory cell.

Magnitude of numbers. The design of each computer determines the magnitude of numbers which can be used in computation. Positive or negative whole numbers are known as **integers**. Integer values are limited by the number of binary digits which a memory cell can hold. To accommodate larger values, and real numbers with fractions, numbers can be stored in a special format called **floating point**, similar to "scientific notation" for numbers. Such values are stored in two parts: a fractional value, known as the **mantissa**, and its **exponent**, represented as a power of 2.

DECISIONS

Sequential processing of instructions does not provide the flexibility which programs need to make decisions and execute alternative paths in the program's logic. The logical unit of the computer's ALU carries out instructions which perform conditional tests and transfer control, or **branch**, to a new program address based on the results of the test.

Logical operations. In addition to arithmetic operations, a set of logical operations are also possible on binary values. The operations "AND", "OR", "XOR" (exclusive OR), and "NOT" are defined according to the rules of **Boolean algebra**. (These operations are more fully described in Chapter 3.)

Conditional tests. Data values stored in the registers of the ALU may be compared to the binary values 0 or 1, or to data values stored in memory cells. The "true" or "false" condition which results from a comparison will cause a specific action to be taken by a conditional instruction.

Program branching. A conditional instruction may place a new program address in the program counter. The Control Unit will branch to this new location since it always determines the next instruction to execute from the address stored in the program counter.

Jump and return. A branch instruction, (sometimes called a **jump**), may save its current address when it transfers control to a new location. The Control Unit can then return to continue executing the original sequence of instructions after the instructions at the new location have been completed.

MOVING DATA

In addition to performing arithmetic and logical instructions, and executing branch instructions to start a new program sequence, the Control Unit may also be called upon to move data values from one location to another. Whether the data moves are between main memory cells, from main memory to auxiliary storage or to input/output devices, the Control Unit activates the appropriate circuitry to move the data as the instructions specify.

SECONDARY STORAGE

Auxiliary Memory

Most computer users require more extensive memory than is provided by main memory in order to securely store large amounts of data over time. A variety of devices are available on modern computers to extend their memory capacity and provide permanent storage for data.

MASS STORAGE DEVICES

Tape drives. Among the earliest of auxiliary storage devices still in use are **magnetic tape** drives. Tapes exist in a variety of widths (1/4 inch, 1/2 inch) and lengths. They can hold large amounts of data and have the added advantage of being portable. Thus, information can be physically removed from a computer, and can be kept in a bank safe, for instance.

Disk drives. An essential mass storage device on modern computers is a **hard disk drive**, which contains a set of disk-shaped surfaces for storing data. Disk drives serve as extensions to main memory, and are used as the permanent storage devices for both programs and data.

Floppy disk drives. Disk drives which read and write small diskettes, known as **floppy disks,** are common storage media for personal computers. Although diskettes can hold less data than hard disks, they have the advantage of being small (typically 3 1/2 inches or 5 1/4 inches), and easily removed from the computer to be stored elsewhere.

CD-ROM drives and Optical disks. Computer designers have used the latest technology to develop new devices with speedier access and large capacities as optional media for data storage. The same technology which produces musical compact disks is used to store read-only (ROM) data, and optically readable disks also provide an easily removable disk with large storage capacity. Such devices are particularly useful for storing large quantities of text information, such as computer manuals.

Removable data storage media, such as tapes, floppy disks, and CD-

ROMs, make it easy to save and protect data, as well as securely transfer data between different computers.

ATTRIBUTES

Data stored on auxiliary memory devices has some important differences from data stored in main memory locations.

Indirect addressing. Although data stored on an auxiliary memory device also have specific addresses, the computer's instructions cannot address the auxiliary memory locations directly. The needed data must first be transferred to main memory where the computer's instructions can access them.

Static storage. The data values stored in auxiliary memory are static, and will remain until new values are written over them. Loss of the computer's electric power will not erase the values stored.

Slower speed. Since data on auxiliary devices cannot be addressed directly, and must be transferred by special circuits, known as **data buses**, into the computer's main memory, the access speed of such data is slower than data retrieved directly from main memory.

DATA ORGANIZATION

Data on auxiliary devices is also stored in binary form, just as in main memory, but some constraints are imposed on its organization by the physical characteristics of the devices. Two primary organizational schemes for data storage are currently used.

Sequential storage. Storage media such as a tape imposes a sequential arrangement on the data contained on it. In order to access any item of information, the tape has to be positioned to the correct spot, and all previous data must be passed by.

Data written on tape is typically ordered into a series of chunks called **records**, and the tape contains **header** information to help locate individual records. Tape mechanisms also recognize physical gaps between records as a way to control read and write operations.

Random storage. Disks of various kinds store their data on tracks which are arranged circularly on disk surfaces, and are further organized into sectors with specific addresses. Descriptive **directory** information is maintained on the disks to speed up the search for specific locations. Disks are known as **random access** devices because data is located directly, not sequentially, as on tapes.

SIZE

Mass storage devices are capable of holding very large amounts of data, often measured in **megabytes** or **gigabytes** (approximately one million and one billion bytes of information respectively). Such large capacities are possible because of technologically innovative media, and the use of intermediate storage buffers to feed slowly accessed data to the speedy RAM circuits of main memory.

INPUT / OUTPUT

A variety of electronic devices exist to transfer information in and out of computers. Input data can be entered by users directly, or may be transferred over telecommunication lines, transmitted from sensing devices, or read from a computer's auxiliary memory. The output results of processing can be temporarily saved as input for other programs, or can be translated and presented to the computer user in human-understandable form.

User Input

INPUT DEVICES

The function of an input device is to accept information entered by a user and to translate it into the binary form which the computer can process.

Keyboard. Computer keyboards are a common means for users to enter data. Keyboards have a layout similar to typewriters, and allow the user to type in alphabetic characters, numbers, and symbols, such as #, $, ", etc. Keyboards typically include some unique keys, such as a **control** key, which causes special action to be taken when the key is pressed.

Mouse. A mouse is a hand-held device which the user manipulates to move a pointer, called a **cursor**, on the computer screen. A click of one of the mouse keys is an input signal to the computer.

Optical and other devices. Optical scanners, such as a **light pen** which reads bar codes on products, or devices which read account numbers from checks, also read and transfer information into the computer. Some computers accept touch on the screen as input, and voice input is an increasingly common option for providing information to computer programs.

Punched cards. The usual means of input for early mainframe computers were 80-column cards in which patterns of punched holes represented coded data. Because faster devices exist today and interactive computing is preferred, punched cards are no longer widely used for computer I/O.

DATA TRANSFER

Data conversion. Before it can be processed, the data entered by a user from a keyboard, or other input device, must be translated into the binary form which the computer understands.

The circuitry of each input device converts the electrical signals of the device into predefined codes in the computer's language. Each of the characters typed in from a keyboard, for instance, is converted into the binary code assigned to it in the computer's predefined character set.

Buffering. Because the speed of the CPU far exceeds the human speed of typing or clicking with a mouse, input data is collected into temporary storage areas called **buffers** before it is transferred to the computer's main memory. This intermediate storage of user input also allows errors to be corrected. Thus a user can delete and retype characters before the information is actually sent to the CPU for processing. (The use of buffers is further described in the I/O section of Chapter 4.)

User Output OUTPUT DEVICES

The function of an output device is to translate the binary results produced by a computer program into a form understandable by humans. An important consideration is the transportability of the output. Although the computer user can view the results on the computer's display screen, it is often desirable to have the output in a "hardcopy" form which can be saved for later review.

Computer screen. The computer's display screen is the most common output medium for interactive computing. The screen is usually the display surface of a **CRT** (Cathode Ray Tube, as in a television set), which is built into output devices such as **monitors** or **VDTs** (Video Dispaly Terminals). Computer screens are capable of displaying text, and very commonly also graphic images.

Printers. Printers have been the most popular output device for computers because they allow the user to walk away with the results of his computation on a piece of paper ("hardcopy"). A variety of peripheral devices for producing printed output are in use. **Dot matrix** printers form each character from a grid of tiny dots, while **ink jet** printers spray a thin stream of ink to form the printed characters. Very high quality printout is produced by more expensive but highly sophisticated **laser printers** which produce characters in many fonts at high rates of speed.

Plotters. Plotters also produce hardcopy output, but are used primarily to produce graphical images, such as charts and drawings. A common feature of plotters (much rarer in printers) is that a variety of colors can be used to distinguish different parts of a picture, such as the segments of a pie chart, for instance. Some plotters produce maps, blueprints, and architectural plans on very large sheets of paper.

Other output devices. Computers can also produce sounds as output signals via special devices, and voice is becoming an increasingly common output medium. Special programs exist which allow users to compose music and play the results directly on the computer.

DATA TRANSLATION

The binary results produced by computer processing must undergo conversion from electronic signals to human-understandable form, whether the output is in the form of text, graphics or sound. A considerable amount of processing may be required to produce the text or image which is presented to the user.

Interfaces. Special hardware devices known as interfaces, typically printed circuit boards which are installed in the computer unit, are designed to handle the complex processing which is sometimes necessary to produce user-friendly output.

For instance, a graphics image on the screen is composed of single dots, known as pixels which must be moved from memory to the screen when the picture is drawn. For such graphics processing, special graphics cards which are complementary to the graphics output device, handle the transfer of the pixel data and its arrangement on the screen.

Buffers. As in the case of input data, information destined for output is collected in buffers before it is sent to an output device. Since output devices are much slower than CPU processing, buffering prevents the CPU from being interrupted by small data transfers. The CPU can send large chunks of data to buffers in rapid bursts, and the output device can process the data at its own slow pace. (A further discussion of I/O buffering appears in Chapter 4.)

Computer I/O

Computer programs also process **input data** which has been created by other programs, and create intermediate **output data** for other programs, which is not necessarily seen by the user. Such transfers typically take place from auxiliary memory devices where intermediate data files can be temporarily stored.

It is also possible to transfer input readings directly from an electronic measurement device, and to send output signals to control another electronic device. Cardiac monitors in a hospital's intensive care unit, for instance, read a patient's heart rhythms from special sensors, and display the heart's activity on a screen, or plot it to a special chart for medical personnel to review.

*Each computer is a collection of electronic devices whose circuits process information and communicate with users. The computer's operations are controlled by a **Central Processing Unit** capable of processing information stored in the circuits of the computer's **memory**. The **CPU chip** decodes a program's instructions from memory, and activates the various circuits that perform arithmetic and other basic operations on data. User input is read by **input devices** such as a keyboard, and the results of computation are dis-*

*played on a screen, or sent to a printer or other **output device**. Disks, tapes, and other **mass storage** devices are available as well for long-term storage of data.*

Central to the design of modern computers is the use of the binary number system to store both programs and data. Chapter 3 covers the binary representation of numbers, text and machine instructions, and the basic operations of binary arithmetic and logic.

3

Binary Data and Machine Language

All *information in modern computers is represented and processed in binary form, as strings of 0s and 1s. The computer's **CPU** decodes binary data in memory as it performs a program's instructions. The simplicity of binary representation, which can easily be represented by electronic circuits, makes the great speed and efficiency of modern computers possible.*

Programming languages provide a method for representing data and program instructions in a form which is closer to human language. However, an understanding of the underlying binary representation of information clarifies the limitations of computing, and is helpful for writing correct and efficient programs.

BINARY DATA REPRESENTATION

Bit

The basic unit of information stored in the computer is a **bit** (derived from **binary digit**), which can represent either a value of 0 or 1. Electronically, each bit is represented by an electronic switch which is either in an **on** or **off** state. The two states allow a bit to be interpreted as **on**, **off** information, **yes**, **no** values, or the digits 1 or 0.

Byte

Because a single bit represents a minimal amount of information, bits are organized into longer groupings in order to represent meaningful data.

A series of **eight bits** in a row is known as a **byte**. A byte is commonly used as the smallest unit of information to represent characters, such as numbers and letters, or other other coded information.

Word

To allow larger goupings of coded data and instructions, many computers organize their memory cells into longer units called **words**. Words can range from 16 to 32 bits in length for most minicomputers and mainframes, but can be as long as 64 bits for supercomputers with complex capabilities. Word length is important because it determines the size of numbers which can be used in computations, and also the extent of memory which can be directly addressed by the computer's instructions.

BINARY NUMBERS

The binary representation of data is closely related to the **binary number system**, and forms the basis of a computer's computational capability.

Counting

Counting in the binary system (base 2) follows the same rules as counting in our familiar decimal (base 10) number system. The decimal system provides 10 digits for counting, while only the 0 and 1 digits are available in binary.

In both number systems, the position which a digit occupies in a number is important, because it implies the power of the base by which that digit must be multiplied. The linear arrangement of the base digits allows us to represent values larger than a single digit. Special rules define how arithmetic is to be performed on these values.

COUNTING IN DECIMAL

The decimal number system provides the digits 0 1 2 3 4 5 6 7 8 9 for counting. When we wish to count past 9, we add a carry of 1 to the position on the left, and reuse the digits to continue counting. Each position in the number signifies a power of 10, such as a hundred or thousand. Each digit in the number must be multiplied by the power of 10 appropriate to its position, and the set of products added together compute the numeric value.

EXAMPLE 1.

In the decimal system, the digits which we would write for the year the Berlin Wall fell, 1989, can be pictured by the following scheme.

10^5	10^4	10^3	10^2	10^1	10^0
0	0	1	9	8	9

This representation corresponds to the arithmetic statement

$$(0\times100000)+(0\times10000)+(1\times1000)+(9\times100)+(8\times10)+9 = 1989 .$$

COUNTING IN BINARY

The same idea is used for binary represenation as for the decimal. For counting, a carry is made to the left whenever we run out of digits. Since now only two digits are available, we have to carry a 1 every other time.

Thus, counting to the number 10 in binary produces the following results.

Decimal	Binary
0	0
1	1
2	10
3	11
4	100
5	101
6	110
7	111
8	1000
9	1001
10	1010

Just as in the decimal system, each binary digit (**bit**) in a binary number represents a power of 2 (the base of the binary number system). A binary value can be converted to its decimal equivalent by multiplying each binary digit with the power of two represented by its position, and adding the products together.

EXAMPLE 2.

(a) The binary number 00011001 can be pictured by the scheme:

2^7	2^6	2^5	2^4	2^3	2^2	2^1	2^0
0	0	0	1	1	0	0	1

which corresponds to the arithmetic statement

$$(0\times128)+(0\times64)+(0\times32)+(1\times16)+(1\times8)+(0\times4)+(0\times2)+1 = 25 .$$

(b) Using the above scheme, the decimal numbers 25, 33, and 128 can be represented by the following binary notation.

0	0	0	1	1	0	0	1	(25),
0	0	1	0	0	0	0	1	(33),
1	0	0	0	0	0	0	0	(128).

(c) Continuing the scheme for counting in binary that was described earlier, the numbers 11 to 20 can be represented by the following binary notation.

	1	0	1	1	(11)
	1	1	0	0	(12)
	1	1	0	1	(13)
	1	1	1	0	(14)
	1	1	1	1	(15)
1	0	0	0	0	(16)
1	0	0	0	1	(17)
1	0	0	1	0	(18)
1	0	0	1	1	(19)
1	0	1	0	0	(20)

Shorthand Notation

The octal (base 8) and hexadecimal (base 16) number systems are often used as a shorthand notation for expressing long binary strings of 0s and 1s.

OCTAL AND HEXADECIMAL

In binary counting, it becomes apparent that a series of three bits represents a number 0 through 7, which are the base digits of the **octal** (base 8) number system. Similarly, a series of four bits corresponds to a base digit of the **hexadecimal** (base 16) number system. The following table shows the relationships.

Binary	Octal	Binary	Hexadecimal
000	0	0000	0
001	1	0001	1
010	2	0010	2
011	3	0011	3
100	4	0100	4
101	5	0101	5
110	6	0110	6
111	7	0111	7
		1000	8
		1001	9
		1010	A
		1011	B
		1100	C
		1101	D
		1110	E
		1111	F

Because we only have 10 decimal digits available for counting, and the hexadecimal system needs 6 more, the alphabetic characters A through F are used to count past 10 in the hexadecimal number system.

With these two sets of equivalences, it is convenient to break a long binary string into shorter octal or hexadecimal representation.

EXAMPLE 3.

(a) The 6-bit binary string

    1 0 1 0 0 1 is equivalent to 51 in octal

      5   1

(b) The 8-bit binary string

    0 1 0 1 1 1 1 0 can be represented as 5E in hexadecimal

      5   E

(c) The 36-bit string 101000110110110011001111011101111101 shortens to 506663173575 in octal, if the bit pattern is partitioned into 3-bit groupings as follows:

    101 000 110 110 110 011 001 111 011 101 111 101

and the same bit string can be expressed in hexadecimal as A36CCF77D, if the binary string is partitioned into the following 4-bit groupings.

```
1010 0011 0110 1100 1100 1111 0111 0111 1101
```

CONVERSION

Conversion from octal and hexadecimal notation to binary, and vice versa is straightforward, once the bit patterns that represent the digits (and the characters A – F) become familiar.

The grouping of bits (by 3 or 4 bits) should always start from the right-most bit, which is known as the **low-order** bit, and the string should be filled with 0 bits on the left in order to complete an octal or hexadecimal digit.

Conversion of values from the octal (base 8), the hexadecimal (base 16) or the decimal (base 10) number system to binary equivalents, involves dividing the values by 2. The series of 0 or 1 remainders resulting from the division form the binary equivalent.

Number Formats

INTEGER

Binary numbers stored as bit strings in a computer memory cell are known as **integers**, i.e., whole numbers. If the stored number is small, the leading bits of the memory cell are filled with 0s.

Sign. In most computer architectures it is common to use the leftmost bit, known as the **high-order bit**, to represent the sign of the number. Typically a 1 in this position of the bit string indicates a negative number, while a 0 implies a positive number.

EXAMPLE 4.

(a) A byte of memory which contains the bit string 00000110 represents the integer value +6.

(b) The bit string 10000110 means that the negative integer value − 6 is stored in the byte.

Size. The magnitude of an integer number which can be stored in a memory cell is limited by the cell's length. If the high-order bit is reserved for the sign, then the maximum number which a cell can hold is a number with 1 bits in all the remaining positions.

EXAMPLE 5.

(a) In a byte of memory (with the high-order bit reserved for the sign), the bit string 01111111 represents the largest positive value which can be stored. In decimal, this is the integer + 127.

(b) In a 16-bit computer word, the maximum negative integer which can be stored is a bit string of all 1s, with the the high-order bit also a 1 to indicate a negative value.

The bit string 1111111111111111 represents the integer value − 32,767 as shown by the arithmetic expansion:

$$(1\times2^{14}+1\times2^{13}+1\times2^{12}+1\times2^{11}+1\times2^{10}+1\times2^9+1\times2^8+1\times2^7+1\times2^6+1\times2^5+1\times2^4 +1\times2^3+1\times2^2+1\times2^1+1\times2^0).$$

FLOATING POINT

An alternate format, called **floating point**, is available in many computers to represent numbers with fractions (known mathematically as **real numbers**). This format also allows much larger values to be stored than is possible with integer format.

Format. The bits in a memory word are divided into three groups, or **fields**, to hold a floating point number. As in integer format, the high-order bit represents the sign of the number. A predetermined number of bits after the sign are reserved for the **exponent** field, and the remaining low-order bits store the fractional part of the number, known as the **mantissa**. The value of the exponent is the power of two by which the mantissa must be multiplied to equal the numeric value represented.

The architecture of each computer determines how many bits are allocated to each of the fields of a floating point number.

In a computer with a 16-bit memory word, for instance, the format might be defined as follows:

SEEEEMMMMMMMMMMM

where S is the sign bit, the Es represent four bits reserved for the exponent, and the Ms define the field used for storing the mantissa.

EXAMPLE 6.

In floating point format, the number 17.625 would be stored as

0110110001101000

where the 4-bit exponent field contains the bits 1101, the 11-bit mantissa field contains the bits 10001101000, and the high-order 0 bit indicates that the numeric value is a positive number.

Radix point. The radix point is the binary equivalent of the decimal point in decimal notation and is always assumed to be located to the left of the mantissa. The binary fraction is stored in **normalized** form; that is, the bit to the right of the radix is always a 1.

In Example 6, the radix point is implicitly defined to be between the exponent and mantissa fields, i.e., between the fifth and sixth high-order bits.

Signs. The **high order** sign bit of the floating point bits represents the sign of the numeric value. As in the integer format, it is typically a 1 for a negative value and a 0 for a positive value.

Since the exponent represents the power of two by which the fractional mantissa must be multiplied, it can be either positive or negative. However, exponents are always stored as positive values without a sign bit, in a form which is sometimes called **excess notation**. A base value is chosen for the exponent, and all exponent values are stored as an offset from this value. The ALU makes the necessary adjustment during floating point computations.

BINARY ARITHMETIC

Basic operations

Arithmetic on binary numbers is done in special **registers** of the **arithmetic/logical unit** of the **CPU** by two basic types of electronic circuits. Circuits for binary addition are involved in every operation, and additional circuits to convert numbers to their two's complement form (described below) are also utilized for subtraction and division operations.

Although the examples below show 8-bit binary numbers, the rules for binary arithmetic are the same no matter how long the computer word.

ADDITION

Rules. The basic rules of binary addition are:

$$
\begin{array}{cccc}
0 & 0 & 1 & 1 \\
\underline{+0} & \underline{+1} & \underline{+0} & \underline{+1} \\
0 & 1 & 1 & 10
\end{array}
$$

Carry. Just as in the decimal system, when a **carry** is generated by the addition operation, a 1 is carried to the left, and added to the other digits in that position.

EXAMPLE 7.

```
(a)     37          00100101
      + 22        + 00010110
        59          00111011
                        ^
                      carry
```

(b)	230		11100110
	+ 15	+	00001111
	245		11110101
			^^^

carries

COMPLEMENT NOTATION

One's Complement. The complement of a binary number is its bit string written with each digit reversed. That is, each 1 in the bit string is written as a 0, and each 0 becomes a 1.

EXAMPLE 8.

(a) The one's complement of the bit string 1000 is 0111.

(b) The one's complement of the bit string 11001100 is 00110011.

Two's Complement. The two's complement of a binary number is defined as the **one's complement** of the number + 1. The following table shows the 4-bit representations of the (decimal) numbers 0 to 10 in their binary, one's complement and two's complement form.

Decimal	Binary	1's complement	2's complement
0	0000	1111	0000
1	0001	1110	1111
2	0010	1101	1110
3	0011	1100	1101
4	0100	1011	1100
5	0101	1010	1011
6	0110	1001	1010
7	0111	1000	1001
8	1000	0111	1000
9	1001	0110	0111
10	1010	0101	0110

EXAMPLE 9.

(a) The two's complement of the binary number 01110100 is

$$
\begin{array}{r}
10001011 \\
+ \qquad 1 \\
\hline
10001100
\end{array}
$$

(b) The two's complement of the binary number 11001100 is

$$
\begin{array}{r}
00110011 \\
1 \\
\hline
00110100
\end{array}
$$

SUBTRACTION

Computers perform binary subtraction by forming the two's complement of the number to be subtracted (the **subtrahend**), and adding it to the value to be subtracted from (the **minuend**). If the resulting operation produces a carry past the high-order (sign) bit, the carry bit is discarded to achieve the correct result.

EXAMPLE 10.

```
(a)    17          00010001
     -  5          11111011   (the two's complement of 5)
       12          00001100
                   ^
```

carry is ignored.

```
(b)   140          10001100
     - 89          10100111   (the two's complement of 89)
       51          00110011
                   ^
```

carry is ignored.

MULTIPLICATION

Multiplication of binary values is performed as a series of additions and shifts by the ALU. The multiplication expressed as 4×5, for instance, implies that four 5s are to be added together. Also, as is shown in the example below, because each position in a binary number represents a power of 2, shifting a 1 bit one position to the left is equivalent to multiplying it by 2.

EXAMPLE 11.

If a computer's ALU has an 8-bit register in which bits can be shifted one position to the left, it can be used for multiplication. Using the notation of Example 2, we can see that the numeric value 12 becomes the value 24 when its bits are shifted one position to the left:

```
2^7   2^6   2^5   2^4   2^3   2^2   2^1   2^0

 0     0     0     0     1     1     0     0    (1×8) + (1×4) = 12
```

becomes

```
 0     0     0     1     1     0     0     0    (1×16) + (1×8) = 24
```

When a value in the register is shifted, the empty position at the low-order end is filled with a 0 bit.

DIVISION

A computer's ALU performs division as a series of subtractions, using the two's complement form of numbers which was described earlier. Since no fractions can be stored in binary integer format, any remainder from an integer division is discarded. That is, the result is **truncated**. In order to work with fractions, programmers can use floating point number formats and operations.

EXAMPLE 12.

Integer division will produce the following results:

(a) $18 / 3 = 6$,

(b) $18 / 4 = 4$ (truncated result).

FLOATING POINT ARITHMETIC

Arithmetic operations on floating point numbers are similar to those performed on integers. However, because of the exponential representation of these values, operations are performed separately on the mantissa and exponent according to the rules of algebra. Floating point division will not truncate the result, and any remainder is retained as a fractional part of the resulting value.

OVERFLOW

Because of the fixed length of memory cells it is possible that computations on binary numbers may result in values that are larger than can be represented in a memory word. This is known as an **overflow** condition, and typically results in an error message.

ROUND–OFF ERROR

Also because of the fixed length of memory words, the complete binary representation of a floating point number's mantissa may not fit into the field set aside for it. As a result, a part of a number's value is lost during computations. The error may be compounded in complex computations where round-off errors occur at several steps of the computation.

Overflow conditions and round-off errors can only be avoided by having an understanding of the range of values used in computations, and by writing a program's steps in such a way that these errors will be minimized.

BINARY LOGIC

*Logical
Operations*

    In addition to binary arithmetic, a computer's ALU also performs logical operations on binary data, which allow the computer's instructions to perform tests and control the sequence of operations.

BOOLEAN OPERATORS

    Four basic logical operations, based on the rules of Boolean algebra, are defined for binary strings. The operations are performed on two bit strings of equal length. Equivalent bits in the two strings are operated on to yield a 1-bit result. Unlike binary arithmetic, there are no carry bits produced by these operations.

    AND operation. The result of the **AND** operation is defined as follows.

```
    1          1          0          0
AND 1      AND 0      AND 1      AND 0
    1          0          0          0
```

EXAMPLE 13.

(a)
```
        0010111
AND 1001001
    0000001
```

(b)
```
        111110000
AND 101010101
    101010000
```

    OR operation. The result of the **OR** operation is defined as follows.

```
   1         1        0        0
OR 1      OR 0     OR 1     OR 0
   1         1        1        0
```

EXAMPLE 14.

(a)
```
        0010111
OR 1001001
    1011111
```

(b)
```
        111110000
OR 101010101
    111110101
```

EXCLUSIVE OR. The result of the **EXCLUSIVE OR** operation (also known as **XOR** is defined as follows:

```
     1          1          0          0
 XOR 1      XOR 0      XOR 1      XOR 0
     0          1          1          0
```

EXAMPLE 15.

(a)
```
        0010111
    XOR 1001001
        1011110
```

(b)
```
        111111111
    XOR 101010101
        010101010
```

NOT operation. The **NOT** operator is applied to a single binary string, and has the effect of reversing each bit to its opposite state. That is, each 0 becomes a 1, and each 1 becomes a 0. In the terminology of logic, this is known as a **negation** operation.

EXAMPLE 16.

(a)
```
    NOT 10001
        01110
```

(b)
```
    NOT 11110000
        00001111
```

MASKING OPERATIONS

Specific bit strings can be used as **masks** to alter other bit strings by means of the Boolean operators. As Example 13.b illustrates, a mask of 111110000 applied with the **AND** operator preserves the first five bits of the operand, and zeroes out the last four bits. Similarly, in Example 15.b, a mask of all 1s applied with the **XOR** operator has the effect of forming a **one's complement** of the operand.

TESTING

True/False conditions. In computer logic, the state of a bit, i.e., whether a 1 or 0, can be tested to produce a logical result of **true** or **false**. A computer's instructions can then make decisions based on the true or false condition of a particular bit in a binary string.

EXAMPLE 17.

The high-order bit of a binary number represents the sign of the number. If the bit is 1, the number is negative, otherwise the value is positive.

The ALU can test for a negative value by testing the sign bit of a number.

Given the 8-bit binary number 10010110, the result of the test will be **true** since the sign bit is a 1. That is, the bit string represents a negative value.

Comparisons. Computer logic also includes the capability of testing bit strings for equality, or determining whether one binary string is less than, or greater than another string. The following notation is typically used for comparison operations:

=	equal to,	<>	not equal to,
<	less than,	<=	less than or equal to,
>	greater than,	>=	greater than or equal to.

The result of a comparison operation is always the logical value **true** or **false**.

EXAMPLE 18.

(a) `00100111   <>   00010111`   is **true**,

because the two binary strings are not identical. The ALU can simply do a bit by bit comparison, in order to determine equality.

(b) `00100111   <   00010111`   is **false**,

since the first 1 bit in the binary number on the left appears earlier than the first 1 bit in the binary number on the right. Because each 1 bit represents a power of 2 in binary notation, the value on the left is larger. The ALU simply needs to scan the bits from left to right to determine which string represents a larger number.

BINARY CODED CHARACTERS

Computers perform a variety of operations on information which does not represent numeric values and does not involve computation. In order to represent other data, such as alphabetic characters, various coding schemes have been developed. Two widely used definitions, **ASCII** and **EBCDIC**, represent each character as a special binary code which can be stored in a byte of memory.

A typical character set includes lower-and upper-case letters, numeric digits, punctuation marks such as ! . ? , and various other special symbols like tab and space. Most of the defined character codes can be printed as output, but some codes are unprintable and are used only as internal signals.

ASCII

ASCII is the character code which the American National Standards Association has adopted, and is an abbreviation for "American Standard Code for Information Interchange." It is a popular code and is widely used on PCs.

The ASCII code represents each character in a 7-bit format:

ZZZNNNN,

where the three Zs are known as **zone** bits, and the four N bits are a binary number.

EXAMPLE 19.

In ASCII, the word Hello would be represented as the bit string:

```
1001000 1000101 1001100 1001100 1001111 .
```

EBCDIC

The EBCDIC code is an 8-bit code which has evolved for IBM and IBM-compatible computers. The abbreviation stands for "Extended Binary-Coded Decimal Interchange Code."

The EBCDIC format includes four zone bits, and four numeric bits:

ZZZZNNNN .

EXAMPLE 20.

The word Hello would be represented in EBCDIC as the bit string:

```
11001000 11000101 11010011 11010011 11010110 .
```

Definitions

Appendix A contains a table with the printable **ASCII** and **EBCDIC** character codes.

MACHINE LANGUAGE

Instruction Set

The architecture of each computer defines a set of instructions to accomplish the operations intended by the designers of the machine. The instructions vary with the complexity of the computer, the speed of its electronic circuits, and the size of addressable memory which has been allocated. All computer architectures include instructions for the following basic operations:

arithmetic and logical operations to be performed by the ALU;

transfers of data between memory locations, special CPU registers, and input/output units;

control of the operation sequence by means of unconditional and conditional jumps to a new program location.

The binary representation of a computer's instruction set is known as its **machine language**.

Instruction Format

Each computer instruction is a specially coded binary string which occupies a series of bytes, or a word, of computer memory. For a particular architecture, an instruction format is defined in which each **field** of bits serves a particular function. These are primarily **op codes** or **operands**.

OP CODES

OP Codes are the binary codes which represent each of the instructions defined for the computer. Thus, if four bits are defined to represent an operation, each 4-bit code will represent a specific instruction, such as a multiply, AND, or data transfer from memory into a register.

OPERANDS

Each instruction also contains other fields which give the specific detail of how an operation is to be performed.

Registers. When the operation of an instruction requires the use of a special register, such as an ALU register in which floating point arithmetic can be performed, the register identification is given in an appropriate field.

Data addresses. Most instructions involve operations on data values. The memory addresses of data values to be operated on are stored in one or more fields of the instruction.

Jump addresses. Some instructions will perform a jump to another memory location, either unconditionally, or as the result of a comparison. The address where the next instruction is to be found is stored in such jump instructions.

Flags. The operation of some instructions may be modified by a special binary flag which is set, or not set, in an appropriate field.

EXAMPLE 21.

A sample computer called EX has instructions defined to be 16 bits long, with the following fields.

```
cccc rr aaaaaaaaaa where
cccc                        is a 4-bit operation code,
rr                          is a 2-bit field reserved to identify a register,
aaaaaaaaaa                  specifies the address of a data value.
```

(a) An operation to load a value from memory location 115 to the arithmetic register 3, would be written:

    0101110001110011

if the binary code 0101 represented the "load" operation.

(b) If the operation code 1001 specifies the shift of a register to the right, then:

    1001100000000010

will shift register 2 two places to the right. In this case, no memory address is referenced, but the number of shifts is stored in the low-order bits of the instruction.

(c) A conditional transfer operation in the EX computer may require two instructions: one to load a memory value into a register, and another to jump if the value in the register is less than zero:

    0101010001000110

will load the value from memory address 70 to register 1.

    1100010011111000

will jump to location 248 if the value of register 1 is < 0 . The operation code for the conditional jump is 1100 in this case.

Assembly Language

The task of writing all the instructions of a program in their binary form would be extremely time-consuming and tedious for programmers. It would be difficult to remember all the binary operation codes and to track memory addresses in binary as well. It would be a frustrating effort to find and correct the large numbers of errors which would result.

A higher-level form of representation, called **assembly language**, is defined for each computer's instruction set to make the programming task easier. Each operation code is assigned an easily remembered mnemonic code, and the other fields of an instruction can also be represented by symbols. Symbolic names can be assigned to the memory locations which a program uses, and the **assembler** which translates the program will assign actual memory cells to the symbols when the program is ready to run.

EXAMPLE 22.

The instructions given in the previous example, might appear as follows in the EX computer's assembly language:

(a) LOAD 3, ROOT

the value stored in a memory location called ROOT is loaded into register 3;

(b) SHR 2,2

the value in register 2 is shifted two positions to the right;

(c) LOAD 1, XYZ
    JLT 1, PART2

the value stored in the memory location called XYZ is loaded into register 1. The value in register 1 is compared to zero and the program jumps to location PART2 if the value in register 1 is less than zero.

*All information is stored and processed in modern computers as a series of 0 and 1 digits, known as **bits**. Bits are grouped into longer 8-bit units, known as **bytes**, to store characters, and into longer **words** to hold numbers and program instructions. A computer's word-size is the basic length (in bits) of its memory cells and depends on the design of its architecture.*

*Numeric data is stored in memory either in **integer** or **floating point** format, and the arithmetic operations performed on numbers follow the rules of binary arithmetic. Logical operations on binary data are also possible, and allow program instructions to make decisions and choose between alternative courses of action. Each computer's design includes a set of instructions to perform its operations. Instructions are stored in memory, just as the data on which they operate, and consist of binary codes that the CPU is able to decode and activate.*

Computers perform their operations at great speeds because electronic circuits can easily represent the two-state binary system. Although programmers usually work in higher-level programming languages, a knowledge of underlying binary representations can be helpful in writing correct programs.

4

System Software

A computer's hardware devices are useless unless there is software to drive their electronic circuits. Programs written to solve user problems, as well as the programs which coordinate the overall activities of a computer system, are collectively known as **software**.

Whether a single user runs a program, or multiple users interact with a computer system, a control program known as the **operating system** must coordinate the activities of its various parts for efficient operation. The letters typed in from a keyboard, or the clicks of a mouse, must be captured and transmitted to the program expecting input. Main memory must be made available to running programs as they request space, and disk storage must be managed so that data can be easily stored and retrieved when needed.

System software manages the computer's various resources and also provides a range of general-purpose services which allow users to write programs and accomplish a variety of computational tasks.

OPERATING SYSTEM

The overall management of a computer system's operation is done by a specially designed program called its **operating system**. It is the function of this important program to coordinate all the activities of the computer and to insure the efficient use of the system's resources.

Operating systems are customized to a particular computer architecture. Two popular operating systems in use today are **MS-DOS** which was designed by the Microsoft Corporation for use on PCs. and the **Unix** operating system, developed at AT&T and available on a wide range of more powerful computers.

Process Control

When a program's instructions are being interpreted by the CPU, all its specific tasks such as computation, reading from a disk or writing to a printer, etc., are known as **processes**. An important function of the operating system is to schedule and monitor all the processes which need the resources of the machine.

SYSTEM BOOT

Boot process. When a computer's power switch is turned on, a process known as the boot process begins to execute. The CPU reads instructions from specific memory locations which **bootstrap** additional program instructions into the computer's memory.

Boot ROM. The first boot instructions are typically stored in ROM memory where they are always available, and the rest of the boot program is usually read in from a fixed address on an **auxiliary storage** device such as a disk. The boot program **initializes** the operating system so that it can begin to accept commands from user programs.

PROCESS STATES

Each process which requires the use of the computer's CPU, memory, or I/O devices undergoes several **states** before it completes its task. A process begins to **execute** when the operating system directs the CPU to decode its instructions. The process is terminated or **killed** when its task is finished or an error which cannot be corrected occurs. Processes also **sleep** when they are suspended by the operating system, either because their allotted execution time is up or because they are waiting for the completion of another process before they can continue.

INTERRUPTS

Because the CPU and I/O devices can operate independently, the operating system can allow different tasks to be executed at the same time. However, when a process such as the task of sending information to an output device is started, the operating system needs to know when the task is finished. Signals, known as **interrupts**, are generated to inform the controlling program that the activity has been completed. The interrupt mechanism allows the operating system to synchronize processes which are executed in parallel.

PROCESS SCHEDULING

Multitasking. Most modern operating systems are multitasking systems which allot a period of time, known as a **time-slice**, for each task waiting to execute. Each task (process) may enjoy a time-slice of only a few milliseconds for its execution before it is suspended and control is given to the next task waiting in the **queue**. However, because modern computers execute millions of instructions per second, each task appears to execute continuously when compared to human reaction time.

Priorities. The operating system **schedules** processes to make the most efficient use of the computer's various resources. A set of rules, known as a **scheduling algorithm**, is designed for each operating system to provide the formula by which the sequence of control is maintained. **Priorities** are assigned to tasks according to the scheduling algorithm or by users. Low-priority processes are often executed in the **background**. That is, time is allocated to these processes only when higher-priority tasks are completed.

Clock. The computer's clock, which controls the execution of each individual instruction, also controls the time-slices allotted to processes. In addition, users or the operating system can schedule a particular process to be executed at a specified time of day.

DAEMON PROCESSES

Processes which are scheduled to run automatically without intervention from users, are known as daemons. These processes perform periodic tasks which are needed to keep the overall system running smoothly. For instance, a daemon process may have the responsibility of checking every 15 minutes whether mail has arrived in the computer over the network. The process may do nothing more than draw a graphical image of a mailbox with its flag raised on the screen, to alert the user to check mail messages.

INTERPROCESS COMMUNICATION

Processes can instruct the operating system to start other processes, and to terminate them as needed. Processes can also communicate with each other by requesting the operating system to pass messages between them. Such mechanisms for **interprocess communication** allow processes to synchronize their activities and to share data. Thus, if a **parent** process receives a message that a task has been completed from a **child** process which it started, it can then send a message to the operating system to terminate the child process.

Memory Management

A computer's **main memory** is one of its critical resources. Each program which executes, including the operating system itself, must be resident in memory before the CPU can execute its instructions. An important function of the operating system is to control the allocation of memory to the various processes which request it.

SHARED MEMORY

Since the operating system is always in control of a computer's operations, a portion of main memory is reserved for its essential processes. The remaining memory is available for other executing programs. In order to minimize the time spent in loading a process into memory when its turn to execute comes, the operating system uses special memory management techniques to determine what to keep resident in main memory, and when to load a new program from secondary storage.

Paging. Typical memory management schemes partition the computer's memory into a set of fixed size blocks, known as **pages**. Page size depends on a computer's architecture, and may be 450 or 1024 memory locations, for instance. A **memory management algorithm** assigns memory pages as they are requested, and keeps track of which process is stored in each page of memory. New processes are loaded into the page blocks according to the priorities of the scheduling algorithm.

VIRTUAL MEMORY

When the CPU is executing a program, it references the physical addresses of memory locations to find the program's instructions and the data values which the instructions specify. These addresses are known as **absolute** addresses, and the total amount of memory which a program and its data require is called its **address space**. It is possible that the address space required by a program exceeds the size of a computer's physical memory. Also, only a limited number of memory pages may be available for a program in a multiprocessing system where memory is shared by many processes.

When a program is translated into machine language (as explained at the end of the chapter), its addresses are generated as if the total memory of the computer were available for it. The memory it requires is said to be its **virtual** address space. The machine language instructions of a program reside on an auxiliary memory device, such as a disk, until it begins to execute. When its turn comes, the memory management routines load segments of it into main memory pages and translate its virtual addresses to the absolute addresses which the CPU can execute.

SWAPPING

The memory management routines must constantly allocate available memory pages to the processes which are scheduled for execution. Space which is no longer used by an active process can be assigned to a new process, but there is often a need for more space than is free. The memory management system may use an area of secondary storage on disk which is set aside as a **swap area** for temporary storage of processes. When a process is pre-empted by another with higher priority, its pages may be

swapped out of main memory until it is rescheduled for its next time-slice. Because the swap area is under direct control of memory management routines, it is much faster to reload process pages from here, rather than from their original program space on the disk.

MEMORY PROTECTION

Because many processes occupy main memory at the same time, there is the danger that errors in an executing program may cause it to access locations outside its address space. It is especially important that essential operating system processes are protected from accidental access. In many computers, protection mechanisms have been designed into the architecture, to help the memory management routines protect each process area from interference.

Secondary Storage Management

One of the major functions of the operating system is the management of auxiliary storage devices, such as the disks which make up its secondary storage system. Except for small computers that rely only on a floppy disk for secondary storage, most computers require a substantial amount of disk space for the permanent storage of programs and data. The space requirements may range from 20 MegaBytes (million bytes) on a small system to a GigaByte (billion bytes) of storage space on a powerful workstation.

OPERATING SYSTEM STORAGE

A specific area of disk storage is usually reserved for the operating system. As the dynamic requirements of processing vary, operating system routines are read from the disk and executed as processes in the same way as user programs. The most active routines may be assigned to specific disk addresses in order to make access to them as fast as possible.

SWAP SPACE

A fixed area of disk space is often set aside as the **swap area** for the memory management system. Program pages are temporarily **swapped out** to this space to make room for a new process which needs main memory pages. The swapped pages are reloaded into main memory from the swap area when the suspended program gets another turn to execute.

The size of the swap area is usually optional, and depends on the size of the computer's main memory. When the swap area is large, it allows more processes to be held in reserve, waiting for their turn to execute.

FILE SYSTEM

The disk space, which remains after the operating system needs are met, is available to hold the programs and data of users. This organized area of storage is known as the **file system**. It is managed by the operating system to allow access to the individual collections of information, known as **files** which have been created by users and programs. (The organization of the file system is more fully described later in this chapter).

I/O Device Control

As processes execute, they need to transfer data to input and output peripherals and auxiliary memory devices. The operating system must control and synchronize the activity of the I/O devices in such a way that processes receive input when they need it, and are able to send results to output devices without slowing down the CPU's operations.

DRIVERS

Each type of I/O device has specialized circuitry for transmitting information. For instance, the electronic signal generated by the "backspace" key on a keyboard causes the previous typed character to be erased, while a "carriage return" character sent to a printer means that the text which follows will be written on a new line. Requests to read data from the disk, on the other hand, must first execute commands to position the disk read/write head in the correct position.

The operating system includes specialized **device drivers** to control the communication with I/O devices. Each **driver** is a piece of operating system software which is designed to communicate with a specific device, to locate data, translate electronic signals to binary representation, and transmit the data to a requesting process. The operating system synchronizes I/O activity by communicating with drivers which handle the actual work of transmitting data.

BUFFERING

Because the interaction speed of humans and the transmission speed of I/O devices is far slower than the speed of the CPU, the data transmitted between I/O devices and memory is collected into **buffers** before it is processed. A **buffer** is a block of memory into which characters are stored as they are received from an input device, or as they are generated before being sent to an output device. Once the block is full, the driver transmits the whole buffer to an executing process in the case of input, or to the device for which output was intended. When an executing process requests I/O activity, the operating system suspends it until an **interrupt** from a device driver indicates that a buffer of data is ready to be transmitted.

SPOOLING

When several processes create data to send to an output device such as the printer, intermixing of data can easily occur without some kind of control mechanism. A technique known as **spooling** is used by operating systems to hold data files in a **spool queue** from which they are scheduled for printing. Whenever a printing activity has been completed, the next file in the queue is scheduled, while new data files can be added to the spool queue.

TERMINAL I/O

In multiuser systems, several users may wish to access the computer at the same time. The operating system maintains a program which waits for an interrupt signal from each line to which a terminal is connected. When a user types, the signal is received, and the communication with the user is initiated. The user must **log in** to the system by typing an approved "account" name to which access permission has been given. Usually, a confidential codeword known as a **password** is also required to verify legitimate access.

Command Language

Users interact with the operating system by giving **commands** which the operating system recognizes. Commands instruct the operating system to perform services for the user, such as running a program, printing a file, or deleting a file. The subsystem which recognizes and processes commands is known as the **command language interface**. In the popular **Unix** operating system, this interface between the user and the operating system is called the **shell**.

FILE SYSTEM

The disk storage devices which make up a computer system's secondary storage are organized into a **file system** to store user programs and data. Each collection of information which is saved on the disk is known as a **file**, and is identified by a **file name** chosen by its creator. Specific commands to the operating system allow users and programs to locate and access the files stored in the file system.

Organization

Operating system routines must be able to locate files speedily in order to make them accessible to users. In a **flat** file system organization, a catalog is maintained which lists the file names with their corresponding disk addresses. This method is not efficient for large systems where a long list of names may have to be searched, and there is the possibility that the same file names might be used by different users. Instead, a more efficient hierarchical organization has been implemented in many current systems. The Apple Macintosh system, DOS operating system, and the more sophisticated Unix operating systems all utilize a hierarchical file system organization.

HIERARCHICAL STRUCTURE

Directories. Individual files are stored in **directories**, which are related to each other in a **hierarchical** fashion, as follows. At the highest level is a directory known as **root** which contains files and/or other directories. These other directories are known as **subdirectories**, and they are said to be at the next lower level than the root. These subdirectories may in turn contain files or other subdirectories, and so on.

EXAMPLE 1.

A hierachical structure is sometimes called a **tree structure** because of its appearance when it is illustrated by drawing line-segments to show containment relationships.

In a **Unix** file system, "/" represents the **root** directory and "etc", "users", and "tmp" are typical subdirectories in root. As illustrated in Figure 4.1 below, there may be additional subdirectories in this hierarchy, with files stored in them.

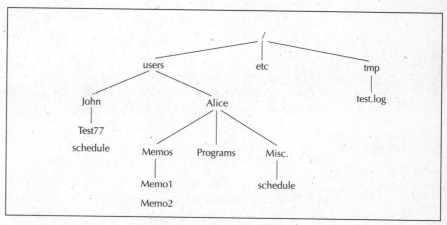

Figure 4.1—File system hierarchy

Path names. In a hierarchical file system, a file can be found only if its location relative to the directory hierarchy is known. In other words, if the file is in a directory contained in another directory, etc., then these relationships must be known, or the file can't be found. The file's **pathname** is a notation which specifies its name, and the directory paths which lead to it. Each file system uses a unique notation for specifying pathnames, as is shown in the example below.

EXAMPLE 2.

(a) For the **Unix** directory structure of Example 1, the following path-names will correctly locate the files.

```
File            Pathname
Memo2           /users/Alice/Memos/Memo2
test.log        /tmp/test.log
Test77          /users/John/Test77
```

(b) In a hierarchical organization, the same file name may appear more than once, as long as the files are stored in different directories. Thus

```
/users/John/schedule
```

will locate the file named "schedule" from the subdirectory "John".

```
and /users/Alice/Misc/schedule
```

will locate the file named "schedule" from the "Misc" subdirectory.

(c) The **DOS** operating system uses somewhat different notation to specify pathnames. The notation

```
C:\DOCS\MEMOS\MEMO23
```

implies that the file "MEMO23" is located in the subdirectory "MEMOS" of the directory "DOCS". The "DOCS" directory is in turn a subdirectory of the root directory C: .

File Operations

USER ACCESS

Users may work with files stored on a system's disk by typing commands to the operating system. Although the specific names of commands may differ from system to system, the basic operations are very similar.

Creation and deletion. Users can create files by typing text into an **editor** or **word processor** program. A **save** command will store the typed information into a file whose name is chosen by the user. A **delete** command will remove a file from the file system.

File manipulation. Users may rename files, copy them, or move files from one directory to another by giving the appropriate commands. A list of the files stored in a directory may be requested, and the contents of a text file may be displayed on the screen. If the file is to be **listed**, that is sent to a printer, a specific print command must be given.

Security. In multiuser systems, protection mechanisms are needed to secure an individual user's files from unauthorized access. In some systems, such as Unix, the creator of a file can specify who may read, write, or execute a file. Users who do not have access privileges will be prevented from working with a file; they can even be prevented from seeing it.

PROGRAM ACCESS

Programs process files by issuing **system calls**. These requests to the file management routines make files accessible and supervise the transmission of data between I/O devices and programs.

File creation. When an executing process wishes to create a file, it must specify a name and request disk space from the file management system before it is able to send information to it.

Open and Close operations. Before a program can read information from a file, or send information to it, a link to the file's reserved storage area must first be set up. An **open** command locates the file in the disk directory and sets up the path to it. When processing has been completed, a **close** command must be issued to inform the file management system that access to the file is no longer needed.

Read and Write operations. To read information from a file, a program issues a **read** request to the file management system. Similarly, a **write** request transmits data which the program has created to an open file. The **read** and **write** commands initiate processes which transmit data between the program and the buffers interacting with the device drivers.

File locks. It is sometimes important to block access to files on a temporary basis, so that one process cannot modify a file until another process is finished with it. A process may request that a file be **locked** during its access. Once the operation is finished, the lock can be released, to allow access to other processes. This is important in airline reservation systems for example, where a transaction must be completed before information is inadvertently changed.

File Structures

PHYSICAL STORAGE

Records. The data which is written to a file is organized into units known as **records**. Each record is composed of **fields** of data such as numbers or characters, and usually has a fixed length. For instance, an 80-character line of text on the screen forms a typical record. Records are further collected together into **blocks** in file buffers, before data is actually written to an output device. Similarly, blocks of data are read from an input device by the device driver, and are stored in an input buffer. The file management routines transmit a single record from the buffer when a read request is received.

The blocking of records allows I/O operations to be scheduled in an **asynchronous** fashion. That is, much slower I/O operations can occur in parallel with fast CPU processes. Since data is always available from buffers, the physical transmission of data does not slow down the computer's overall operations.

Sequential storage. On tape media, blocked records can only be written sequentially, one after the other. A blank space, called an **inter-record gap** is left between records to indicate their separation, and a special **end-of-file** character is written after the last record to indicate where a file ends.

Random Storage. On disk media, records are stored on tracks on the disk's surfaces, but sequential order is not important. Storage is said to be **random** because any record can be accessed just as easily as any other.

ACCESS METHODS

Sequential access. On tape media, records can only be read sequentially. Just as on a video tape, a record written near the end of a tape can only be read if all the previous records have been passed by. A tape must be rewound, if records at its beginning are read after the tape has already been positioned past them.

Direct access. Any record stored on a disk can be accessed directly once its physical address is known. Directories are maintained on the disk surfaces to indicate where the records of a file are stored. Once a record address has been determined, the disk's read/write heads can be positioned to the correct spot, and the data is immediately available.

Indexed access. A common technique to make data in very large files quickly accessible, is the use of a **key field** as an index to a file. A directory which contains all the possible **keys** is maintained, and the address of the relevant record is associated with each key. Once a key is located in the directory, direct access to the information is possible.

EXAMPLE 3.

In a video rental store, a customer's telephone number may serve as a key into the file containing information on all customers who are authorized to rent videos. When a new rental is about to be recorded, the rental program will use the customer's telephone number as the key into the customer directory. The directory entry will contain the disk address where the customer's data is stored, and the information can then be read and displayed on the screen.

SOFTWARE SUBSYSTEMS

In addition to the routines which directly control the operations of a computer, operating systems also include subsystems which provide other important functionality to users. These general-purpose programs enable users to write their own programs and accomplish other important tasks at a higher level, so that they do not have to know and understand all the technical details for getting their job done.

Language Translators

Programs which translate user instructions from a higher-level language to machine language, and load them into memory for execution, are an essential part of system software.

COMPILER AND LOADER

A **compiler** processes the program statements written in a programming language and translates each program step into binary machine language codes which the computer's CPU can decode and execute. A program called a **loader** then transfers the translated code to main memory for execution, and inserts absolute memory addresses into all instructions which reference memory locations.

INTERPRETER

An **interpreter** reads and translates program statements dynamically and executes them in main memory immediately. Although the load step is eliminated, interpreted programs execute more slowly than programs which are first compiled and then loaded for execution.

Some languages, such as FORTRAN, Pascal, and C, were designed to be compiled then loaded and executed. Programs written in BASIC, LISP, or Prolog are more typically interpreted.

A program called a **debugger** is sometimes provided to help programmers find programming errors or **bugs**. A debugger program interacts with an executing program and enables the programmer to interrupt the running program in order to examine changing memory locations, or to trace the paths which are followed through the program's instructions.

Networking Software

Computer systems are often connected to a network in order to communicate with each other and share data files. Because the technical details of data communication between computers can be quite complex, programs are provided to enable users to accomplish their tasks in a networked environment at a higher level. For instance, users can work remotely on another computer, or send a data file to it by giving special commands which activate the network programs.

EXAMPLE 4.

Users on networked computers often have a **Mail** program available which enables them to send electronic mail (**e-mail**) over the network. The details of routing a typed message over networks which span miles, or even continents, are too complex for each user to program individually. However, a user can simply type a message with the recipient's e-mail address, and the Mail program will automatically route the message over the network.

Libraries

Operating systems often include libraries of preprogrammed code which can be accessed directly by a user's program to accomplish specialized tasks. For instance, in a computer system capable of displaying graphic images, the machine code required to draw a figure may be tedious to program. However, if a library of graphics routines is available, the user need only specify a high-level instruction to access the code which will perform the task.

Utility Programs

Operating systems also provide a set of additional utility programs to help users do their work more easily.

EDITOR

All systems need to provide a way for users to enter text into files which will later be used for processing. An **editor** program is usually available to interact with the user to read in information typed in from the keyboard. Editors also allow users to modify the typed text and to save it in the system's file system.

SORT

It is often useful for users to be able to sort data stored in their files. Preprogrammed sort routines allow users to sort data files without having to understand sorting algorithms or write the sorting programs.

The available utility programs vary with the design of each operating system and its intended uses. A user's interaction with the system is simplified when preprogrammed routines are available for common tasks.

APPLICATION PROGRAMS

To accomplish specialized computing tasks on a computer, users may write their own programs, or they may run **application programs** which have been developed to solve specific types of problems. **Word processors** are available for creating documents and **spreadsheet programs** help solve a variety of business problems on PC's. **Database** programs help manage large amounts of information on both small and large computers, and specialized application programs to do statistical calculations or finite element analysis may be available on engineering workstations. The use of preprogrammed software eliminates a great deal of work and enables users to concentrate on the problems they wish to solve on the computer.

Application programs run under the control of the operating system, just as all other programs. They must be written to interact with the operating system so that their memory requirements and I/O activity can be managed to produce the results desired. For this reason, each application program is uniquely tailored to a particular operating system, and must be modified if it is to be **ported** to run on another machine with a different architecture.

*T*he *programs which run on a computer system are collectively known as* ***software***. *A computer cannot funtion without a program loaded into its memory which is being interpreted by the CPU. In addition to the applications programs which are written to solve a user's specific problems, each computer system includes a primary program known as its* ***operating system***. *This is the supervisory program which initiates and controls the operations of the computer's various parts and the interactions with the computer user.*

The main tasks of the operating system are to monitor the various ***processes*** *which are executed by the CPU, and to allocate the resources of the computer, such as memory, when requested by a running program. The operating system also controls data transfers to and from I/O devices, and manages the* ***file system*** *on disks where user programs and data are stored. All user programs run under the control of the operating system, and various* ***subsystems*** *such as compilers and utility programs are also available to the computer user.*

5

Solving Problems on Computers

*B*efore a computer program can be written to solve a problem on the computer, all the needed steps of the solution must be understood and defined. The plan for the program must include the sequence of operations to be performed by the machine's instructions, the organization of data which is needed, and an understanding of the desired results and the inputs available.

The development of **algorithms**, the step-by-step plans for solving problems, is an important task for every programmer. An algorithm may be relatively straightforward for a program whose inputs and outputs are well defined and the computations are sequential, such as the generation of an employee's paycheck. For complex problems, the specification of algorithms is a major part of the problem solving process. Design techniques which permit large programs to be developed in a modular fashion, or help to focus the solution on the efficient organization of large amounts of data, allow software to be developed for very complicated problems. Today's airline reservation systems, for instance, or the programs which control space shuttle launches, are major computer applications which could not be accomplished without well-defined algorithms.

ALGORITHM DEVELOPMENT

***Algorithm
Definition***

An algorithm is a specification of the series of steps which must be followed in order to solve a problem or accomplish a task.

Algorithms can be specified for all kinds of problems, not just those which will be solved on a computer. For example, new cameras usually come with instructions which describe the sequence of steps for loading film. Similarly, the instructions for filling out the Federal Income Tax Form 1040 give an algorithm for determining how many exemptions a taxpayer may claim. In each case, the task can be successfully completed if the sequence of steps is followed.

General Programming Algorithm

A computer program consists of instructions that perform a series of operations on data which it accepts as input in order to produce the results desired as output.

The general algorithm for the specification of a computer program can be represented by the following high-level diagram.

Input ---> { Processing } ---> Output

Based on this general algorithm, a useful approach for developing the steps of a solution is to answer the following questions:

(1) What output is desired from the computer program?
(2) What processing (computations or other operations) must be done in order to produce the output results?
(3) What input data is needed in order to perform the computations? Once satisfactory answers to these questions are provided, the algorithm for the computer program can be defined and the instructions written in a programming language.

EXAMPLE 1.

The algorithm for a program converting Fahrenheit temperature values (F) to Celsius degrees (C) could be expressed as follows.

F --> { apply F to C conversion formula } --> C

It is clear that the ouput desired is a Celsius temperature value, and that a Fahrenheit value must be supplied as input. However, the program cannot be written until the correct conversion formula is known:

$$C = 5/9*(F-32).$$

With this additional information, the program can now be written.

ALGORITHM REPRESENTATION

Pseudocode

The steps of an algorithm are sometimes written in English in a short-hand form called **pseudocode** which provides a high-level description of the operations to be performed. There are no rules for writing pseudocode; its purpose is to summarize the steps of the solution and to make the logical sequence of a program clear.

EXAMPLE 2.

A professor who is about to write a program to assign grades to the students in his Data Structures course might express his final grade algorithm in the following pseudocode:

locate a student's scores

|

IF there are > 6 quiz scores
THEN keep only the highest 6 scores

|

compute the average quiz score

|

compute the average homework score

|

IF the midterm exam was a make-up
THEN reduce the exam score by 10%

|

compute the student's course grade

|

post the student's course grade

This pseudocode algorithm defines the sequence of steps which must be followed to calculate a student's final grade for the course. The algorithm implies that the output of the program will be the final grade, and that a student's quiz scores, homework scores and midterm exam score, are the input values needed for the calculation. The algorithm also indicates two decisions that must be made about the quiz scores and the midterm exam score.

The outlined steps are a good guide for writing the program, but do not provide enough detail for the complete solution. The professor must still supply the actual formula that will be used to compute the grade, and must know how to compute an average score. Also, for the program to be useful, the program steps must be repeated for every student in the class.

To specify the problem solution more completely, the details of the final grade calculation, and an indication of the repeated steps could be included in the pseudocode description.

Flowcharts

Because many problem solutions involve decisions and repeated steps, known as **looping**, a more graphical representation of a program's algorithm is often useful. Such pictures of a program's logic are called **flow charts** and typically use the symbols shown in Figure 5.1 to represent process steps and the flow of control.

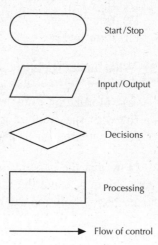

Start/Stop

Input/Output

Decisions

Processing

Flow of control

Figure 5.1—Symbols used in flow charts to represent process steps

EXAMPLE 3.

Automatic Teller Machines or ATMs are an easy way to access one's bank account, especially to withdraw money after hours when the bank is closed. As a first step for generating an algorithm for the program controlling an ATM, we can provide the answers to the questions of the general programming algorithm:

(1) What results (output) are desired from the program?
Answer:
(a) Money (withdrawal).
(b) Transaction statement.
(c) Display of account information.

(2) What processing must be done?
Answer:
(a) Verify the validity of the ATM card being used.
(b) Access the user's account information.
(c) Determine the type of transaction to be made.
(d) If a withdrawal, determine how much is wanted.
(e) If a withdrawal, determine if there is enough money in the account.

(f) If the withdrawal is okay, then instruct the money mechanism to slide out $20 notes.

(g) If a deposit, determine how much is being deposited.

(h) Activate the mechanism which opens the drawer for the deposit envelope.

(i) Update the user's account with the transaction information.

(j) If an inquiry only, display account information.

(k) Print receipt.

(l) Return user's card.

(3) What input data is needed?

Answer:

(a) Information from the user's ATM card.

(b) User's account information.

(c) Requested action and dollar amount.

Now that the general information about the problem's processing has been determined and the inputs and outputs understood, the algorithm for this problem's solution can be represented by the **flowchart** in Figure 5.2.

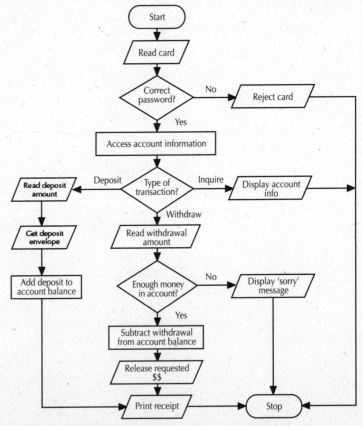

Figure 5.2—ATM program flow chart

Decision Trees

Many problem solutions include decisions whose results will control the flow of a program's operations. The decisions may sometimes be quite complex and can easily lead to programming errors if they are not properly implemented. A pictorial representation known as a **decision tree** can serve as a useful guide for writing the correct algorithms.

EXAMPLE 4.

A telephone company bases its rates for long distance calls on the time of day and day of the week when a call is made. The decision tree graph in Figure 5.3 represents the rules for long distance charges. It can serve as the guide for writing the program statements to compute the charges for long distance calls.

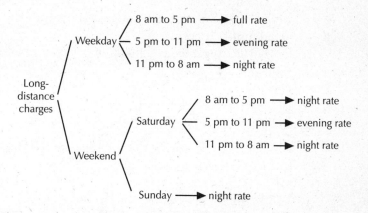

Figure 5.3—Decision tree graph of rules for long-distance telephone call charges

DESIGNING MODULAR SOLUTIONS

Computer programs can be written more efficiently, tested more easily, and maintained with the least effort if they are designed as a set of modules which function together as a whole. Modular design allows the programmer to focus on a small part of the solution at a time, and to build the total program by incrementally combining completed sections of code. Modular design is especially important for complex software projects where teams of programmers develop individual programs which must ultimately interact as a seamless whole.

Top-Down Design

An effective approach to finding modular solutions for complex problems is to first identify the major functions which must be performed by the program. Once the high-level functionality has been identified, each function can then be analyzed and divided into subfunctions. These can be further subdivided until the tasks of the individual program modules can be easily defined.

EXAMPLE 5.

In order to write a program to prepare Federal Income Tax returns, the highest level functions of the program can be defined as follows.

(1) Compute adjusted gross income;
(2) Compute deductions;
(3) Compute credits;
(4) Compute tax or refund.

Although this subdivision does not contain enough detail to develop an algorithm for each function, it is a useful first step. Each of the functions can be analyzed independently according to current IRS rules, and subdivided further if necessary.

For instance, the computation of adjusted gross income consists of the following two tasks.

(A) Compute income; and
(B) Compute adjustments to income.

Furthermore task (A), the computation of income, can be defined even more specifically as the following.

(a) Compute wages;
(b) Compute interest & dividend income;
(c) Compute capital gains;
(d) Compute business income;
(e) Determine and compute other miscellaneous income; and
(f) Add together all income amounts.

STEP-WISE REFINEMENT

The process of analyzing the functional modules at each level of the **top-down** approach is known as **step-wise refinement**. At each stage of analysis the definition of functionality is made more specific, until algorithms for individual program modules can be defined.

EXAMPLE 6.

Using the idea of step-wise refinement, a program module can be defined for task (1)(A)(b) of Example 5 to compute interest and dividend income. The pseudocode algorithm for this computation may be expressed as follows.

read interest amount from each "1099-IN" form
and add to interest sum

|

read dividend amount from each "1099-DIV" form
and add to dividend sum

|

add sum of interests and sum of dividends
and pass result to tax computation module

|

print"Schedule B" form with interest and

dividend information

STRUCTURE CHARTS

The hierarchy of a modular program solution can be shown pictorially in a **structure chart**. The chart can guide the overall development of the program because it displays the modules needed and their relationship to each other.

EXAMPLE 7.

The structure chart in Figure 5.4 shows the high-level modules defined in Example 5 for developing a program to prepare Income Tax returns.

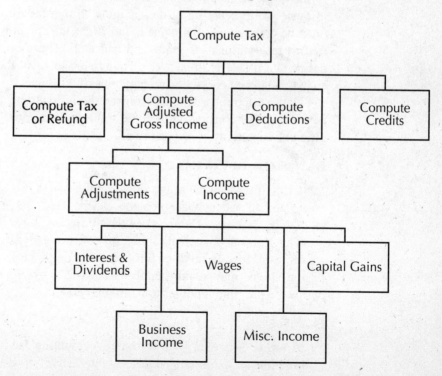

Figure 5.4—Structure chart for program to prepare income tax returns

MODULE ATTRIBUTES

In many cases, there is more than one way of structuring the program into modules. When deciding on a solution, it is important to consider those characteristics of modules which affect ease of development and maintenance of the program.

Coupling. Program modules are said to be **coupled** when they depend on each other. One module may control another, or several modules may share data. It is good programming practice to design modules which are **loosely coupled**. That is, the connections between modules should be minimized and the interfaces between modules should be as simple as possible. If modules are relatively independent and cannot affect the operation of other modules, changes to one module are less likely to cause errors in other modules.

Cohesion. Each program module should be **cohesive**. That is, it should be designed to accomplish a single well-defined task, so that the complexity of its code and its connections to other modules are reduced. Again, fewer programming errors will be made if the functionality of a module is easily understood and relatively independent of other modules.

Data-directed Design

For many program solutions, the organization of large quantities of data is as important as the anlysis of the operations which are to be performed. In an application such as an airline reservation system, for instance, the processing of data is quite straightforward. Airline schedules must be created and maintained, and flight information needs to be modified as reservations are made and canceled. These operations are easy to define, but it is a far greater challenge to organize all the flight information so that it can be accessed from hundreds of terminals.

Data structure oriented design methods focus on the organization of data as a major consideration in the solution of the problem and in the definition of operations to be performed.

DATA FLOW DIAGRAMS

Diagrams which show the flow of information are an important tool for understanding and solving problems where large amounts of data must be processed. The typical elements of a **data flow** diagram are shown in Figure 5.5.

The flow of data in the diagram can be analyzed to define the data structures needed to hold the information. The processing steps represented by the circles may require analysis and step-wise refinement in order to define the program modules to be implemented.

EXAMPLE 8.

A cruise line with state-of-the-art computing facilities wants to make information on its scheduled cruises interactively available to clients who access their computer. The data flow diagram shown in Figure 5.6 repre-

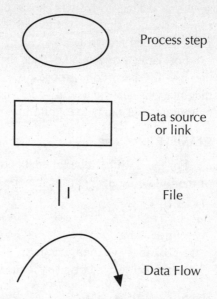

Figure 5.5—Typical elements of a Data Flow Diagram

sents the overall data and operations which must be implemented to respond to a client's query about scheduled cruises.

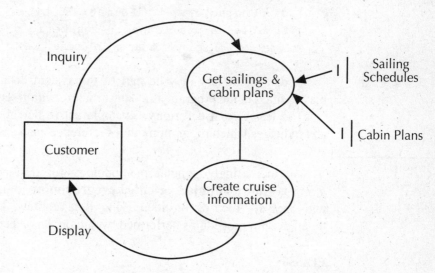

Figure 5.6—Data Flow Diagram for customer query

DATA DICTIONARY

A data dictionary is a useful tool for summarizing the individual data items which will be represented in a program. An entry in the dictionary specifies the name by which the data item will be known, the type and range of values that are valid, where the data item is stored, and which program modules access it.

For large projects, the data dictionary helps to ensure uniformity in the use of data, and exposes contradictions and duplications. The data dictionary is also a useful guide for implementing the data structures in a program, and can help to minimize errors when program changes are made.

EXAMPLE 9.

For the Sailing Schedule data collection of the previous example, some of the following data entries may be defined.

```
Data Element: Cruise      Description: Cruise identifier
   Type: Character        Format: 8 bytes
   Allowable values/ranges: Alphabetic and numeric characters
   References: Display, Update, Marketing

Data Element: Start       Description: Date of embarcation
   Type: Date             Format: mm/dd/yy
   Allowable values/ranges: 01/01/93 to 12/31/95
   References: Display, Update, Calendar, Marketing

Data Element: Ship        Description: Name of cruise ship
   Type: Character        Format: 16 bytes
   Allowable values/ranges: Alphabetic characters
   References: Display, Update, Calendar, Cabin Plan, Marketing
```

A data dictionary may be part of the system documentation only, or may defined in the program as a data structure with fixed length fields.

The less formal descriptive example above documents the data items and indicates which program modules reference each one.

Object-Oriented Design

An increasingly popular methodology for designing computer programs is known as **object-oriented programming**. In this approach, problem analysis focuses on identifying data entities, known as **objects**, together with procedures performed by and on the objects.

CLASSES

Objects are represented as data structures with a defined set of attributes. They are organized into a hierarchy of **classes** where all objects belonging to a class share the same attributes. Each class of objects **inherits** attributes from those classes which are superior to it in the defined hierarchy. Thus each individual object contains its own unique attributes together with all those which it has inherited.

METHODS

Associated with classes and individual objects are procedures, known as **methods**, that have knowledge about the objects and are able to operate on them. Processing is done by activating the methods which operate on the objects.

ADVANTAGES

Object-oriented methodology has several advantages, especially for large programs. Once an object's data structure and its methods have been programmed, the other parts of the program do not need to know anything about the internal structure of the object. This technique of **information hiding** allows different parts of the program to be implemented independently and reduces the possiblity of inadvertent interaction errors.

Object-oriented methodology also makes incremental programming possible. Because the objects are independent, it is easy to add new objects and methods to a class hierarchy. When a program grows, the previously implemented modules do not need to be re-tested because they are self-contained and thus not affected by the new additions.

EXAMPLE 10.

A car rental company may choose to orient its database and billing program around object-oriented design. Its class hierarchy could consist of categories of cars available for rental as shown in Figure 5.7. Individual

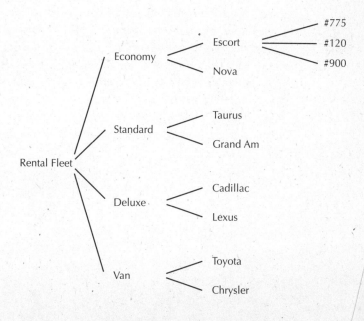

Figure 5.6—Rental car data base

cars could be represented by data objects that contain its attributes, such as style, number of doors, type of transmission, etc.

In the above hierachy, the **Economy** class may be defined to contain cars with standard transmission and the daily rental rate of $19.95. All **Escorts** may be blue two-door models. However, a car in the fleet always has its own unique odometer reading.

With these class definitions, rental car #900 in the fleet is a blue Escort two-door model with standard transmission, costs $19.95 per day to rent, and has an odometer reading of 2550 after its last rental. It has inherited its color, rental price, body and transmission type from higher levels in the object hierarchy, but has its own unique odometer reading.

If the details of an actual rental, such as the date of rental and the customer's name, are added to a car's data structure, then a method could be programmed to determine the cost of rental and generate a bill. When a specific car is returned after a rental, the return method would be activated to generate the final bill by scanning the car's data structure.

Similarly, a very general procedure could be written to generate a report of all the cars rented from the fleet, by processing the data objects in the whole fleet hierarchy. When a new car is added to the fleet, a new data object must be created for it and inserted in the class hierarchy, but none of the processing programs need to be changed.

A well-defined solution algorithm is necessary for all programs if they are to be programmed efficiently and reliably. Problems differ in character, and the best solution is not always obvious until some effort is put into analyzing the problem and determining the requirements of the solution. It is always necessary to know what output is desired and what input data must be available. The actual steps of the solution may be developed by applying the techniques described in this chapter. The organization of data is just as important to the design as the determination of the processing steps needed. The method of modular design is fundamental to the whole software development process which is discussed in the next chapter.

6

Programming and Software Engineering

*The process of translating a problem's solution into instructions that a computer can process is called **programming**. The process usually includes the design of an algorithm for the solution, and the testing of the program to make sure that it gives correct results. When large programming projects are undertaken to produce complex software products, many activities must be managed to ensure successful results.*

*The discipline of managing large software projects which require teams of programmers is known as **software engineering**. The analysis and design techniques described in Chapter 5 are an important part of the software engineering methodology. Additional important activities which must be managed during the development process are described in this chapter.*

SOFTWARE LIFE CYCLE

The overall process of developing software is usually called the **software life cycle**. It typically includes the following phases.

(1) Analysis
(2) Design
(3) Implementation
(4) Testing
(5) Maintenance

Although there may be variations in the way that software projects are managed, these phases represent essential and unavoidable activities in the production of usable and reliable software.

Analysis

PLANNING

The first step for any software project is to analyze the problem to be solved. The scope of the solution must be determined and a plan defined which will serve as a foundation for the algorithms to be designed later.

For large computerization efforts, economic considerations are likely to play an important role. The planning may include decisions about hardware purchases and programming resources that will be needed to complete the project successfully. It may also be necessary to analyze current manual procedures and use the data flow analysis methods described in Chapter 5 in order to determine how they can best be converted to computer programs.

REQUIREMENTS

The goal of the analysis process is to determine the user requirements for the software. In order to design programs that produce desired results, there must be a thorough understanding of the needs of the people who will use the software.

SPECIFICATIONS

Once the requirements are determined, they should be written as a set of detailed **specifications**. These written **specs** will serve as the foundation for the software design and they are the standard with which the results of the software are compared.

Design

ALGORITHM DEVELOPMENT

The design phase of the software development process involves using the methods described in Chapter 5 to design the software solution. Algorithms are developed to produce the results required by the specifications. Program structures are determined and data organizations are defined during this stage of the development process.

DESIGN DOCUMENTATION

The solution plan should be documented to help programmers implement the program modules. Individual program modules may be represented by pseudocode or graphical aids such as flow charts, and data flow diagrams may be used to outline the solution algorithms.

Implementation

The implementation phase consists of translating the software design into computer-readable instructions. This activity is generally known as **programming**.

CODING

The actual work of writing computer instructions in a computer language is called **coding**. Most programs are written in a **high-level language** (described later in this chapter), although it is sometimes useful to write programs in **assembly language**, which is closer to the computer's basic instruction set.

Programs are coded in the form of **statements** which instruct the computer on what operations it must perform. Each statement must be written according to specific rules of the chosen programming language, known as its **syntax**.

TRANSLATING

After a program has been coded in a high-level language, its statements have to be translated into machine language. Either a program known as an **interpreter**, or one known as a **compiler**, is used for this step.

Languages such as Basic are processed by an **interpreter** that translates individual statements as it reads them and executes them immediately. A programmer can easily modify an interpreted program to try a new variation, but interpreted programs tend to be less efficient because the machine code that is generated is not optimized.

Other languages, such as Pascal, must go through a two-step translation process. Program statements are first translated by a **compiler** into machine instructions, which are then transferred to the computer's memory by another program known as a **loader**. Only then can the program be **executed** by the computer's CPU (as described in Chapter 2). Although compiled programs involve an extra step in the translation process, they are optimized during compilation for speed and memory use.

DEBUGGING

Because there are many possibilities for human error when programs are written, they usually do not operate correctly when first executed. Programming errors must be found and corrected in a process known as **debugging**.

When program statements are not written correctly, the compiler cannot complete the translation and will produce a message that it found a **syntax error**. The programmer must correct such errors and try the compilation again until it succeeds.

Even when a program compiles successfully, it may still produce incorrect results. Errors may be the result of faulty logic or of incorrect data specifications. The programmer must find and correct the errors (known as **bugs** in programming jargon). **Debugging** is an iterative process which involves correcting program statements, recompiling and loading the code, and executing the program again to determine if correct results are produced.

Many compilers include a useful subsystem known as a **debugger** to assist in the task of finding errors. A debugger allows a programmer to trace the path of control and examine memory locations as the program executes.

DOCUMENTING

An important part of the programming step should be the inclusion of **comments** in the program statements to indicate what the various sections of a program are intended to accomplish. When program logic is complicated, it is easy for the programmer to forget what was intended by a particular section of code. It is even more difficult, and sometimes very time-consuming, to understand another person's program if the code has not been well documented.

Testing

A planned strategy for testing the finished program modules is an essential part of the software life cycle.

Although debugging of program modules as they are coded is a natural part of the programming process, it cannot be assumed that they produce correct results just because they execute.

Program modules must be exercised by **test cases** with varying input data to ensure that the expected results are reliably produced. It is even more critical to thoroughly test programs which consist of many modules that must interact and function together.

UNIT TESTING

The correct operation of individual modules must be assured before a set of interdependent (coupled) modules can be tested together profitably. Otherwise it becomes very difficult to isolate and track errors to individual faulty modules.

Black box testing. Program modules can be tested by ignoring their internal logic, but focusing instead on the input data which a module accepts and the results which it produces. Test cases can be designed to input valid as well as invalid data, and the module's output can be examined for correctness. If expected results are not produced, the program statements must be analyzed to locate the errors, and the corrected programs tested again.

EXAMPLE 1.

At the Internal Revenue Service, an Income Tax program includes a module which prints a refund check if a taxpayer has paid more tax than he owes. It is important to test the module with varying tax data to make sure the computations are done correctly. A check for $00.00 or –$150.00 cannot be considered correct output, and would probably lead to a very confused taxpayer.

Although $0.00 may be a correct result of the computations, the program should check for this result, and not print a check in this case.

White box testing. A different approach to testing a program module is to focus on its control logic, and ensure that all possible decisions and program branches are tested. In this approach, test cases are designed so that selected input data will exercise as much of the program logic as possible.

EXAMPLE 2.

Another module of the Income Tax program determines the amount of the standard deduction for a taxpayer. The computation for this deduction depends on whether the taxpayer or spouse are 65 years of age or older, or blind, or both, and on the filing status of the taxpayer.

In this case it is important to test all the valid combinations of the deduction criteria to confirm that the deduction is correctly computed. The program's internal logic must be known in order to design appropriate test cases for this module.

INTEGRATION TESTING

When computer programs consist of interdependent modules which share data or control each other, it is important to design tests that will determine whether the modules interact correctly with each other. After the individual modules are judged to be reliable, the modules are combined to determine whether they produce correct results when they work together.

The goal of integration testing is to ensure that interfaces between modules have been implemented correctly. That is, test cases must be especially designed to check out situations where data and/or control is not correctly transferred between modules.

REGRESSION TESTING

Whenever programs are corrected because of errors found in testing, there is always the danger that the corrections may introduce new errors in code that has already been tested. To ensure that this does not happen, it is necessary to run a standard set of tests (often called a **test suite**) on previously tested modules whenever corrections are made.

This method of **regression testing** helps to assure that programs remain reliable at every stage of the modification process.

Maintenance

When software is used over an extended period of time, its maintenance costs could become very large in relation to the original development cost. Once software is turned over to its users, errors are still likely to be found and must be corrected. Programs must be modified when requirements change; moreover, it is common for users to request enhancements, once they become familiar with the operation of programs.

It may be necessary to modify only sections of code, or the original solution must be redesigned to adapt to a new situation. The process could be especially difficult when the people who have maintenance responsibilities are not the same as those who designed the solution and wrote the original programs.

The need for eventual maintenance must be considered at each stage of the software life cycle. Extensive documentation, well-designed independent program modules, and thorough testing are all good software engineering practices that will make the maintenance phase of the software development process manageable.

EXAMPLE 3.

The computerization of a new university veterinary hospital is an example where software engineering techniques can provide a disciplined approach for managing a large software project. In order to produce the complex software which will reliably help manage the operation of the hospital, the software life cycle needs to include the following activities.

(a) Analysis

In order to computerize the hospital's operations, a great deal of analysis and planning must take place before programs to produce bills and store medical records can be written.

Current procedures must be studied and decisions made about which departments of the hospital need access to the computerized system, and what kind of information must be available at each location. Before the hospital's cashier can produce a computerized bill for the Airedale patient "Hector," it is necessary to know how the services provided will be tracked, what the fee for each service will be, and what the bill will look like.

As the analysis is completed, detailed specifications should be written. These should show what a screen full of information must look like for the hospital pharmacist for instance, and what format the final bill must follow to be printed on the three-part forms currently used.

The planning process might include a cost-benefit analysis of which computer harware should be purchased. Also, a suitable programming language must be chosen for the project.

(b) Design

Once the requirements are determined, the algorithms for the overall solution must be developed. During this phase, a design for the organization of the large amount of data which must be maintained is as important as plans for the program modules to be implemented. The design documentation for the hospital's software might include the following.

(1) A structure chart showing the program modules that must be developed for the hospital pharmacy, operating room, cashier's office, large and small animal admitting desks, etc.

(2) A data flow diagram indicating how a patient's service charges flow to the cashier's office, and where the patient's medical record is stored.

(3) A pseudocode algorithm outlining the computations for the final bill.

(c) Implementation

During the implementation phase of the project, the programming staff will code the program modules for each of the functions which were designed. These include a module that prints the bill when a patient is discharged, a module to update the pharmacy's inventory when a prescription is filled, and a data-entry module for the small-animal clinic to enter a new patient's information into the medical records data base.

(d) Testing

The testing phase of the project must include the debugging of individual program modules, as well as the design of a test suite. The reliability of the software cannot be assured until program modules are thoroughly tested both individually and in combination with each other.

If a correct final bill is to be produced, all the data from the various hospital clinics must flow correctly to the common data base, and the billing program must use the correct fees for services and do accurate calculations for the total charges.

(e) Maintenance

Software maintenance will be an on-going process for the veterinary hospital. Programs must be corrected if errors are found during use, and it will be necessary to modify fee schedules as the hospital's services change. It should also be possible to extend the software if a new clinic is added to the hospital. All such changes should be considered as the software is designed, so that future maintenance becomes an easily managed activity.

PROTOTYPING

A very effective step in the development of many software projects is the creation of a **prototype** of the final program for evaluation purposes. It is often difficult to define all the requirements during the analysis and design phase because users do not necessarily know what features they want in new software. A prototype is a trial version of the software which users can try out in order to identify difficulties before the implementation is complete.

Prototypes are usually limited versions of the final programs, and might not be thoroughly tested. It is important to develop a prototype as quickly as possible so that comments from users can influence the final design. It is as important to capture positive reactions as negative ones, so that useful features will be incorporated in the final version. The prototyping process is often iterative. A particular version is changed and refined after user comments, and then presented again for users to evaluate.

For the veterinary hospital of Example 3, it would be helpful to develop a prototype of the data-entry program which accepts new patient input. Hospital receptionists are sure to have suggestions when they actually get a chance to evaluate the program which they will be expected to use daily.

PROGRAMMING LANGUAGES

The choice of a programming language for implementation is one of the important steps during the early phases of the software life cycle. Numerous high-level languages are available on today's computers to make programming easier than writing code in the machine's own binary instruction set.

Although all programming languages must undergo translation, there are variations in the languages which allow different approaches to problem solving.

Assembly Language

The programming language that allows a computer's binary instructions to be manipulated in symbolic form is known as **assembly language**. More meaningful **mnemonic codes** are assigned to the computer's operations, and symbols known as **identifiers** represent memory locations.

Because of its direct relationship to a computer's instruction set, assembly language allows very close control of a computer's operations and efficient utilization of its memory. It is especially useful for applications where fast response time and program efficiency are critical, as for instance in the computer-controlled fuel injection system of a sportscar.

A major disadvantage of assembly language programs is their lack of portability. They are closely tied to one machine's architecture and cannot be easily translated to run on another machine. They are also more tedious to program because of the need to express all operations in low-level detail.

Procedural Languages

Today's most common programming languages allow programs to be written as procedures describing the steps of the solution. They allow operations to be expressed at a higher level, in a form closer to the problem than the machine's basic instruction set.

Procedural languages generally allow the following.

(1) Control of the sequence of operations to be performed. Conditions can be tested to activate different paths in the program's logic, and sections of code can be easily repeated.

(2) Expression of mathematical formulas to instruct the computer to perform arithmetic operations.

(3) The direction of data movement between data storage, input/output devices, and different parts of the program.

(4) Definition of individual data values and their organization.

Although the popular procedural languages share the same basic functionality, each has its own unique features which make it especially suitable for solving certain classes of problems.

FORTRAN

One of the earliest high-level languages, FORTRAN (FORmula TRANslator) was designed to process mathematical equations efficiently. It is well suited for computational tasks and is still widely used for scientific computation. Although it has been extended since its original design, it is limited in its description of data, and is not as well suited for the more modern techniques of structured programming.

COBOL

The COBOL (COmmon Business-Oriented Language) language is another early language which is still widely used. It was developed for data processing applications, such as payroll programs, where large files of character data are manipulated. COBOL programs are verbose because of the English-like syntax, and the language also lacks the useful features of more modern languages.

ADA

The Ada language was developed for the U.S. Department of Defense in the late 1970s to provide some uniformity to the large amount of software developed for defense systems. It is a complex language and includes features allowing tasks to be executed concurrently. This makes it especially useful for real-time applications where a computer controls the system, such as a missile, in which it is embedded. Ada also includes features that support software engineering techniques, such as modular design. It has been successfully used in commercial applications as well as military ones.

BASIC

The BASIC language (Beginners' All-purpose Symbolic Instruction Code) was developed at Dartmouth College by John Kemeny as an introductory programming language. The language is widely used on personal computers and includes especially good handling of character data. Because of its limited features, it is not well suited for development of structured and modular programs.

PASCAL

The Pascal language was also designed as a teaching language by Niklaus Wirth at the ETH in Switzerland. It has become a very popular high-level programming language for software applications because it was designed to embody the advanced techniques of structured programming and data abstraction.

The syntax of the language allows programs to be organized into well-defined modular units which control the program's execution. The extensive data defintion capabilities of the language allow data to be organized into structures that hide the complexity of the organization and allow the data to be manipulated at a higher level.

Part II of this book outlines the basic principles of programming in the Pascal language.

C

The C language is a versatile language which allows experienced programmers to write programs at a level closer to assembly language than many of the other high-level languages. That is, the programmer can manage the computer's memory efficiently and manipulate bits and bytes directly if necesary. The C language is useful in the development of system software because it allows direct control of a computer's basic functions.

Special-Purpose Languages

4GL

The **Fourth Generation Languages**, or **4GLs**, were the next major phase of language development after the popular procedural languages had been developed in the 1960s and 1970s. They are oriented to express problems at a much higher level, with the details of the actual solution controlled by the language translation process. As a result, language users can concentrate on the problem to be solved, without worrying about programming details.

A variety of 4GLs are in use for different types of applications. For example, the **SQL** language is used to processes data from large data bases, and **GPSS** was designed as a language for the simulation of large systems.

ARTIFICIAL INTELLIGENCE LANGUAGES

The development of programs intended to imitate human reasoning is known as **artificial intelligence**. The languages used to solve AI problems include features which allow relationships between symbolic data to be expressed, and provide mechanisms for searching and comparing data to arrive at a solution.

LISP. The LISP language is one of the early high-level computer languages, and is widely used to process symbolic information. It has been used to develop programs which play chess, translate languages, and do symbolic mathematics.

LISP programs are written as sets of functions which call each other to perform specific tasks. The details of data representation are hidden from the programmer, but the processing of lists of character data is a special feature of the language.

Since LISP programs are interpreted rather than compiled, they can easily be modified as they are developed.

Prolog. The Prolog language has been popular in Europe and Japan for AI programing. The language is uniquely based on formal logic, also known as **predicate calculus**.

A Prolog program consists of statements which express the relationship of information expressed as symbols. The language contains a powerful built-in mechanism which searches for a solution by comparing the sets of relationships expressed in the program.

OBJECT-ORIENTED LANGUAGES

Smalltalk. The Smalltalk programming environment was developed in the 1970s to explore the ideas of object-oriented programming described in Chapter 5.

The language allows data objects to be defined and classified according to the attributes they share. Rules of inheritance are defined for the objects, and custom procedures known as methods are attached to each object. A Smalltalk program executes by activating the various methods which process the information contained in the objects.

C++. The C++ language is a set of extensions added to the C programming language to enable the definition and classification of data objects. The procedures to manipulate objects can be programmed in the conventional C language. The extensions to the language allow problems to be solved in the object-oriented style.

All programming projects must go through the various stages of the software life cycle in order to produce reliable software. Analysis of the problem to be solved is essential if the results are to match the needs of the people who will use the software. The choice of an appropriate programming language and attention to good design practices will produce programs that are efficient, and can be easily tested and maintained. Thorough testing is essential to ensure that programs produce correct results.

Large software projects are notorious for delays and cost overruns. A disciplined approach to all the phases of the software development effort is essential in order to deliver reliable and maintainable software on schedule.

PART II—PROGRAMMING IN PASCAL

Pascal *is one of the most popular high-level computer languages in use today. It was developed by Niklaus Wirth in 1971 as a language for teaching the basic concepts of programming and is the introductory programming language for many computer science students. It is also widely used for writing application programs, especially on computers which run the Unix operating system.*

The following chapters outline the core functionality of Pascal, and illustrate the rules for writing correct programs.

7

Programs and Data

A Pascal program consists of **statements** *expressing the actions to be performed by the computer to solve a problem. Each statement performs a specific function in the program. The Pascal programmer must understand the functions provided by the statements and know the rules for writing them correctly. The grammatical rules of the Pascal language are known as its* **syntax***.*

To allow the Pascal compiler to translate a program's statements correctly into machine instructions, the program must follow a prescribed format. It is also important to describe what data the program will use and how it is organized, so that sufficient memory is reserved by the compiler. The organization of a Pascal program and the statements used to specify the program's data requirements are described in this chapter.

PREPARING PASCAL PROGRAMS

A Pascal program is prepared by typing its statements into an **editor** program. The editor allows the programmer to correct errors, and saves the program on the disk when requested. The completed program is then translated by a Pascal **compiler** into machine language, and the translated code is transferred into the computer's main memory by another program called a **loader**. The compiled Pascal program is then ready to **run**. That is, its machine language instructions can be interpreted and executed by the CPU.

A compiled program may be run as many times as desired. However, if errors are found and must be corrected in the Pascal statements, the whole cycle of editing, compiling, and loading must be repeated before another run can be attempted.

PROGRAM FORMAT

A Pascal program must be structured according to the rules of the language. It consists of a **program heading**, a **declaration** section, and a **program body**. The heading identifies the statements which follow as a Pascal program, and the declaration section provides information to the compiler about the program's data. The program body is often called the **main program**, and contains the statements which will be executed. It may activate executable **subprograms**, which are also defined in the declaration section.

EXAMPLE 1.

```
(* Sales Tax Computation *)
Program SalesTax (Input, Output);
(* Declarations *)
   const  Rate = 5.75;
   var  Amount, Total : Real;
(* Main program *)
begin

   WriteLn  ('Enter amount of sale: ');
   ReadLn  (Amount);
   Total  :=  (Amount * Rate) + Amount;
   WriteLn  ('Total charge with 5.75 % sales tax = ', Total);
end.
```

Heading

The program heading is the first statement of a Pascal program. It names the program and identifies external files referenced, but not defined in the program. The program heading of Example 1 names the program **SalesTax** and specifies that files named **Input** and **Output** are used.

FORMAT

Program name (Input, Output);
Program is a reserved Pascal keyword which must appear as the first word of the program.
name is the name chosen by the programmer to identify the program.

( ) enclose the list of external file names.

Input, Output are predefined file names for the program's input and output operations.

; must appear at the end of the statement.

Declarations

The declaration section of the program identifies and defines the data and subprograms used by the program. The data types available in Pascal, and rules for declaring **constants** and **variables,** are described in this chapter. The declaration of more complex **data structures** is described in Chapter 8. Chapter 12 describes the definition and use of **procedure** and **function** subprograms.

Declaration statements are said to be **nonexecutable** because they are not translated into machine instructions. Rather, their function is to provide information about data and memory requirements for the compiler's translation process.

Program body

The statements appearing in the program body form the **executable** part of the program. They are translated by the compiler into machine instructions to be executed by the CPU when the program is run (as is described in Chapters 2 and 3). Chapters 9 through 12 describe the functions of executable Pascal statements which may appear in the main program and subprograms.

FORMAT

```
begin
   statement;
   statement;
end .
```

The begin and end keywords must enclose the statements of the program as is shown.

A . (period) must terminate the program.

STATEMENTS

Each statement must be written according to its Pascal syntax, which may include reserved words and punctuation.

Keywords. The syntax of some Pascal statements includes predefined words, known as **keywords**. These words are reserved by the Pascal language and may not be used for other purposes. The reserved word **Program** which must appear as the first word of a program heading is an example of a keyword.

Separator. Each statement must end with a ; (semicolon), to separate it from other statements. A statement may continue over more than one line.

Punctuation. Punctuation marks and other symbols, such as ( ) := , are required by the syntax of some Pascal statements.

Blanks. Spaces (blank characters) may appear anywhere in the text of a Pascal statement to make its parts more readable.

SYNTAX DIAGRAMS

The rules which have been defined for each Pascal statement can be represented by a diagram, known as a **syntax diagram**. Many Pascal textbooks include the complete set of syntax diagrams which define the Pascal language.

PROGRAM STYLE

Comments

Comments are phrases included in the program's text to explain the functions of different sections of code. Comments can remind the programmer what was intended, and are especially useful when others need to understand a program's logic. Comments must be enclosed by a pair of **delimiters**, which may be the { } or (* *) symbols. The Pascal examples which follow illustrate the use of (* at the beginning of a comment, and the *) symbol at the end.

Indentation

Many Pascal statements, such as data declarations, have complex structures which can make a program difficult to read and understand. Indentation of parts of a statement can be used to group together meaningful sections of the code. Indentation does not affect the translation process because spaces are ignored by the compiler, except when included in character data (as described below). Indentation to make statements clearer is illustrated in many of the examples which follow.

DATA DEFINITION

An essential part of writing a program is a step to determine what data the program will use and how it will be organized. Whether the needed data are numbers, text, or predefined Pascal values, they must be defined in the declaration section of the program so that their internal (binary) representation can be determined, and sufficient memory will be reserved for them.

Data Types

The Pascal language provides more choices than most programming languages for defining data, but a description of all the options available to the programmer is beyond the scope of this book. This chapter and Chapter

8 describe the basic **data types** and **data structures** defined by the Pascal language.

Definitions to describe numeric data, text characters, and the logical **True** and **False** values, are built in to the Pascal language and are usually called the **scalar data types**.

NUMERIC DATA

The Pascal language has two built-in data types for representing numeric values: **integers** and **real numbers**. These definitions correspond to the two basic binary representations of numbers which are described in Chapter 3.

Integer type. Numeric values are known as **integers** when they represent whole numbers and are written as numeric digits without a decimal point. Pascal includes a built-in data type named **Integer** for declaring integer data.

An integer written in a Pascal statement may be preceded by a + or − sign, but may not contain any characters other than numeric digits.

EXAMPLE 2.

(a) The following are valid Pascal integers.

      46   +855   0   −125000   77   1

(b) `$ 125,000` is not a valid integer number because it contains the non-numeric characters **$** and **,** .

(c) `100%` and `#37` are not valid integers because they contain the special characters **%** and **#** .

(d) `.99995` is not a valid integer because it includes a decimal point.

Integer values are stored as binary numbers in the computer's memory (as described in Chapter 3). Because they typically occupy a single memory word, arithmetic operations on integers are faster than on real numbers.

The size of a computer's memory word determines the maximum value which can be represented by an integer. For many computers (with a 16-bit memory word) the maximum integer value is 32767. Pascal includes a pre-defined constant **MaxInt** which contains the maximum integer value.

Real type. Numeric values which are written with a decimal point and may include a fractional part are known as **real** numbers. Pascal includes a built-in data type named **Real** for declaring real data.

A real number written in a Pascal statement must contain a digit before and after the decimal point. It may be preceded by a + or − sign and may include a **scale factor** (described below). It may not contain any characters other than numeric digits.

EXAMPLE 3.

(a) The following are valid Pascal real numbers.

```
    0.0    3.05    0.667    -0.000002    +19980.0
```

(b) `7,000,000.00` is not a valid real number because it contains two commas.

(c) `.9875` is not a valid real number because it does not include a digit before the decimal point.

(d) `$29.95` is not a valid real number because it includes the special character **$** .

Real numbers are stored in memory in floating point format (as described in Chapter 3). The minimum and maximum real values which can be represented depend on the size of the exponent and mantissa fields reserved in a computer's memory word. Real number computations are more complex than integer operations and can therefore take more time. However, real numbers are important in computations because they can hold fractional values and can represent much larger and smaller numbers than integers.

Scale factors. When a number is very large or contains such a small fraction that many zeros are used to write it, a **scale factor** can be used as a shorthand notation for expressing the value. This is often known as **scientific notation** or **floating point** notation.

In Pascal, the letter E followed by an optional + or − sign and the scale factor can be used with **Real** values to shorten the expression of very large and very small numbers. The scale factor represents the power of 10 by which the numeric fraction must be multiplied.

EXAMPLE 4.

Number	Scientific notation	Pascal
(a) 199000000	$199 \times 10^{+6}$	9.0E+6
(b) .00000345	$.345 \times 10^{-5}$	0.345E-5

CHARACTER DATA

Character data are represented in Pascal by enclosing a sequence of characters in a set of apostrophes (single quote marks). That is, the ' symbol appears at the beginning and end of a character value.

Char type. Pascal contains a built-in data type named **Char** to represent a single character from the computer's base character set.

Upper and lower case letters, numeric digits, special symbols, and even the blank (space) character may appear in character data.

The ASCII character set (defined in Appendix A) is a common character set used by many computers. Each character will be stored in the computer's memory as the special binary bit string which has been assigned to that character and will occupy one byte of computer memory (as described in Chapter 3).

EXAMPLE 5.

(a) The following are valid data values of type **Char.**

`'b'`   `'M'`   `' '`   `'6'`   `'%'`

(b) The following do not represent valid **Char** data:

`X`   `"6"`   `$1`

because they are not written as single characters enclosed in a pair of apostrophes.

Strings. A sequence of characters enclosed in a pair of apostrophes is called a **string**. Pascal does not include a built-in data type for defining string data. Instead, such character data must be declared as **arrays** of type **Char.** The declaration of strings as character arrays is described in Chapter 8.

EXAMPLE 6.

The following are examples of valid Pascal string data.

(a) `'Wall Street Journal'` is a string of 19 characters.

(b) `'9/7/1967'` is a string of 8 characters.

LOGICAL DATA

Boolean type. The Pascal language includes a special **Boolean** data type to handle program decisions. Boolean data can only have the two values: **True** and **False**. These values may appear directly in program statements, just as numeric and character data. Operations on Boolean data are described in Chapter 9.

EXAMPLE 7.

(a) `TRUE` and `false` are valid Boolean data; capitalization of any letter does not alter the value.

(b) `'true'` and `*false*` are not valid Boolean values. Unlike character data, Boolean values must not be enclosed by apostrophes or other characters.

CONSTANTS

When numeric, Boolean, or character data values appear in Pascal statements they are known as **constants** because the value which they represent does not change during the program's execution.

EXAMPLE 8.

(a) The Pascal statement

```
Sum  :=  12 + 45;
```

will always compute the sum of the two integer values 12 and 45 and store it in a memory location named **Sum**.

(b) The Pascal statement

```
WriteLn ('HAPPY NEW YEAR !');
```

will always write the character string which represents a new year's greeting.

Constants are also known as **literals**, and their appearance in a program statement is said to be an **implicit** declaration of their type.

DATA DECLARATIONS

Data values stored in the computer's memory and used by a program can be given a name, known as an **identifier**. Identifiers are declared in the declaration part of a Pascal program where the type of data that they will hold is defined. Identifiers can be associated with **constants**, which do not change their value, or **variables**, whose values may change as the program executes.

Identifiers

The names chosen for identifiers must follow the following Pascal rules.

(1) An identifier must begin with an alphabetic character. It may be of any length, but most Pascal compilers use only the first eight characters of the identifier.

(2) An identifier can contain only alphabetic characters and numeric digits. Small and capital letters are allowed, but special characters may not be used.

The names chosen for identifiers should be meaningful to the programmer in order to make the program easier to understand. Unique names should be chosen for different data values. The use of a particular identifier will always access the same memory location which has been reserved for it.

EXAMPLE 9.

(a) `Longitude   LATITUDE,   and  f`   are valid Pascal identifiers.

(b) `new*value    7eleven` may not be used as identifiers because they do not follow the Pascal rules.

Constants

If the same constant value will be used in several places in a program, it can be given a unique name, and its value can be defined **explicitly** in the declaration section of the program.

CONSTANT DECLARATION FORMAT

const

identifier = value;

..

identifier = value;

const is a reserved Pascal keyword which begins a constant declaration.

identifier is a name chosen for a constant. It must follow the rules for identifiers described above.

= must appear between the identifier and its value.

value may be any valid **Integer**, **Real**, **Char** or **Boolean** value. **;** must separate constant definitions.

DEFINITION

(a) Each definition associates a constant with a name. Sufficient memory is reserved to hold the constant.

(b) The constant value is substituted for every appearance of its name in a Pascal statement.

EXAMPLE 10.

The following declaration defines two constants.

```
const

    Interest = 8.75;

    Percent = '%';
```

The floating point number 8.75 is stored in a memory word named **Interest** and the code for the % character is stored in another memory word named **Percent**. These values will be substituted wherever the identifiers appear in program statements.

EXAMPLE 11.

The following statements declare constants of each of the four basic Pascal data types:

```
const
    Quarter   =   4;          (* Integer *)
    Version   =   'A';        (* Char *)
    AuditStatus   =   FALSE;   (* Boolean *)
    InitialBalance   =   0.00; (* Real *)
```

Variables

The (* and *) pairs enclose a comment, as was described earlier.

Just as constant values can be identified by a name, other memory locations which hold data can be associated with a name by the declaration of an identifier. Because data values may vary in these locations, they are called **variables**. The declaration of a variable must specify the type of data which will be stored in the memory reserved for the variable.

VARIABLE DECLARATION FORMAT

var
    list of identifiers : **type**;

    ..

    list of identifiers : **type**;

var is a reserved Pascal keyword which begins a set of variable declarations.

list of identifiers is a list of names chosen to identify variables of the same data type. The identifiers must be separated by commas.

: separates a list of identifiers and its data type.

type may be one of the basic Pascal data types: **Integer**, **Real**, **Char**, or **Boolean** .

DEFINITION

(a) Each identifier listed in a **var** declaration is defined to have the data type specified for the list in which it appears.

(b) Sufficient memory is reserved for each identifier to hold a data value of its declared type.

EXAMPLE 12.

The following three variables are declared.

```
var
    Months : Integer;
    Payment : Real;
    Status : Boolean;
```

Unlike constants, no values will be assigned to variables when they are declared. Values are assigned to variables by executable statements of the program.

EXAMPLE 13.

A program which calculates the charges for international telephone calls might include the following variable declarations:

```
var
    CountryCode ,  Minutes :  Integer;

    Rate, Charge  : Real;
```

The identifiers **CountryCode** and **Minutes** are declared as variables to hold integers. Dollar amounts can be stored in the **Rate** and **Charge** variables because they are declared as real numbers which can hold fractions (i.e. cents).

EXAMPLE 14.

The Pascal declarations below define the constants and variables for a program which will convert a traveling student's cash in dollars to the equivalent amount in French francs and Spanish pesetas. The program uses the exchange rates of 4.997 francs per $, and 107 pesetas per $.

```
Program Convert (Input, Output);
const (* exchange rates *)
   Frate = 4.997;
   Prate = 107.0;
var (* cash amounts *)
   MyCash, MyFrancs, MyPesetas : Real;
```

If the program stores the dollars to be converted in the variable **MyCash**, the equivalent francs and pesetas can be computed and stored into the variables **MyFrancs** and **MyPesetas** by multiplying the dollars with the respective constants representing current exchange rates.

When exchange rates change, only the constant declarations need to be changed; the calculations will still be correct.

DATA ASSIGNMENT

A value can be assigned to a variable by an executable Pascal **assignment statement**.

FORMAT

> **variable := data value**;

> **variable** is a previously declared identifier.

> **:=** is a special Pascal symbol known as the **assignment operator**.

> **data value** is a valid Pascal constant, variable, or **expression** (described in Chapter 9).

EXECUTION

The data value on the right of the **:=** operator is stored into the memory location reserved for the variable which appears to the left of the operator.

EXAMPLE 15.

A Pascal program which calculates the refund to be paid to employees who use their own cars for company business might contain the following statements.

```
(* Variable declarations *)
var
   Miles, Days : Integer;
   Rate, Refund : Real;
(* Assignment statements *)
   Miles := 740;
   Rate := 0.25;
```

The declaration statements define four variables for the calculations, and the assignment statements assign the integer constant 740 to the variable **Miles**, and the real constant .25 to the variable **Rate**.

EXAMPLE 16.

Since **Miles** and **Rate** were declared as **variables**, they may later be assigned new values.

```
Miles := 1020;

Rate := 1.10;
```

That is, the previous value in **Miles** is replaced with the integer 1020, and **Rate** will be replaced with the new real value 1.10 .

EXAMPLE 17.

Variables may appear on the right side of an assignment operator.

```
Miles := WeeklyMiles;

Rate := WeeklyRate;
```

When these statements are executed, the value stored in the variable **WeeklyMiles** will be stored in the variable **Miles** and the value of **WeeklyRate** will be stored in the variable **Rate.**

Execution of the assignment statements will not remove the values from the variables on the right of the :=. Rather, the values will be copied from the variables on the right to the variables on the left of the assignment operator.

*A*ll data which is processed by a Pascal program must be defined as one of four basic data types. Numeric values can be represented by **Integer** and **Real** data types, character data by the **Char** type, and a special **Boolean** data type represents logical values.

Known data values may appear literally as constants in program statements, or they may be given symbolic names and defined in **const** declaration statements. Symbolic names may also be assigned to memory locations known as **variables** to hold changing data values during program execution. All variables must appear in declaration statements in which their data types are defined. Actual data values may be assigned to variables in executable Pascal assignment statements which are further described in Chapter 9.

8

Structured Data

Variables are named memory locations which a Pascal program uses to hold its data. Integer or real numbers, charater data, and Boolean values may be stored in single variables, but it is often desirable for a program to process whole groups of related data without assigning a name to each individual value. To make operations on data collections such as lists of names or tables of numbers easier, Pascal allows data to be grouped into **data structures** which can be accessed with one variable name.

Data may be grouped as **arrays** in which each value is of the same type, or as **records**, which can contain values of several types. Each array or record data structure must be defined in the declaration section of the program. The declaration causes a variable name to be associated with the data structure, and an appropriate number of memory locations to be set aside (allocated) for the data. Individual data values can be accessed as needed from an array or record, and some operations can be done on the data structure as a whole.

NUMERIC ARRAYS

A collection of related numeric values of the same type (**Integer** or **Real**) may be defined in a Pascal program by the declaration of an **array variable**. The declaration must specify the size of the array, and the type of data which will be stored in the array.

One-dimensional Arrays

An array which holds a list of values is said to be **one-dimensional**. Any individual item of the array (called an **element**) can be accessed by a single **subscript**, which serves as a locator for the value stored in the array.

An one-dimensional array is declared as follows in the next section.

ARRAY DECLARATION FORMAT

var identifier : **array [subscript range] of type**;

var, **array**, **of** are reserved Pascal keywords.

identifier is a name chosen for the array. It must follow the rules for identifiers described in Chapter 7.

: and **[ ]** separate fields of the array definition.

subscript range specifies the range of values which may serve as subscripts for the array. The notation 1..n means that the integers 1 to n may be used as subscripts.

type is the data type of the elements of the array, usually **Integer**, **Real**, **Char**, or **Boolean**.

DEFINITION

(a) Memory is reserved for a collection of data identified by the name chosen for the array.

(b) The number of elements stored in the array is determined by the definition of the subscript range. Elements of the array are accessed by a subscript which falls within this range.

(c) Each value stored in the array is assumed to be of the type that is specified.

EXAMPLE 1.

The following declaration defines an array called **Quizzes** to store eight integer quiz scores for a student in a mathematics class:

```
var Quizzes : array [1..8] of Integer;
```

The notation [1..8] specifies that the integer numbers 1 to 8 can be used as subscripts to access the individual values stored in the array.

Two-dimensional Arrays

When a collection of data represents a table or matrix of values, a **two-dimensional** array can be declared. The declaration must specify the number of rows and columns for the array.

Two **subscripts** are required to access data from a two-dimensional array: the first to specify the row, and a second subscript to specify the column location of the data element.

ARRAY DECLARATION FORMAT

var identifier : **array[row-subscript range,column-subscript range] of type**;

var, array, of are reserved Pascal keywords.

identifier is a name chosen for the array. It must follow the rules for identifiers described in Chapter 7.

: and **[ ]** separate fields of the array definition.

row- and column- subscript range specify the range of values which may serve as subscripts for the array. Both a row and column specification are required for a two-dimensional array.

type is the data type of the elements of the array, usually **Integer**, **Real**, **Char**, or **Boolean**.

DEFINITION

(a) Memory is reserved for a collection of data identified by the name chosen for the array.

(b) initions of subscript ranges. The first field specifies the subscript range for the **rows** and the second for the **columns** of the array. Elements of the array are accessed by pairs of row and column subscripts which fall within the ranges specified.

(c) Each value stored in the array is assumed to be of the type specified for the array.

EXAMPLE 2.

An array variable named **Stocks** could store the performance data of a trader's ten favorite high-tech stocks on the NASDAQ exchange:

```
var Stocks : array [1..10,1..3] of Real;
```

The notation **1..10** specifies that the array has ten rows which can be referenced by the integer subscripts 1 to 10. The **1..3** notation specifies that the integers 1 to 3 can be used to specify a column location for an element of the array. Since the array has 10 rows and 3 columns, 30 memory locations will be reserved to store the stock data. Each row represents one stock's data, with the low price stored in one column, the high price in another column, and the net price change in a third.

Although it does not matter which columns are assigned to the high, low, and change values, the program must be consistent once a scheme is adopted.

Numeric arrays may hold either **Integer** or **Real** values, but not a combination of both types.

Array Type Definitions

In Pascal, a **type** statement can define a particular array structure. The name given to the type can later be used to declare array variables.

FORMAT

type array type = array [subscript range] of element type;
type is a reserved Pascal keyword.

array type is an identifier chosen as a name for the array structure.

The remaining fields follow the array declaration syntax described above.

DEFINITION

(a) An array structure definition is associated with the type identifier.
(b) The identifier may be used to define the structure of array variables declared in **var** statements.

EXAMPLE 3.

The statements below define two array structures **Scores** and **Grades**, and two array variables **Quizzes** and **MidTerms**.

```
type
    Scores = array [1..8] of Integer;
    Grades = array [1..30,1..2] of Real;
var
    Quizzes, Homework : Scores;
    MidTerm, Final  : Grades;
```

Quizzes and **Homework** are defined as one-dimensional arrays to hold a student's quiz and homework scores, for which memory for 8 integer values is reserved. Sufficient memory will be set aside to hold a table of 60 real numbers for the **MidTerm** and **Final** arrays. These two-dimensional arrays can hold the exam grades for 30 students, where each student's grades are in one row. The first column of each array might hold the first semester's grades, while the second semester's grades are stored in the second column.

EXAMPLE 4.

A Hawaiian island's tourist bureau could use a Pascal program to track the island's average monthly low and high temperatures for use in its advertising. Three variations of array declarations to hold integer temperatures are shown below.

```
(a) var
        Lows : array [1..12] of Integer;
        Highs : array [1..12] of Integer;
(b) type
        Temps = array [1..12] of Integer;
    var
        Lows, Highs : Temps;
(c) var
        Yearly Temps : array [1..12,1..2] of Integer;
```

(a) and (b) use a one-dimensional array to hold the average low temperatures, and another to hold the average high temperatures for each month. In (a) the array variables are declared directly with their structures, while (b) defines an array type **Temps** which is then used to declare the two temperature arrays.

(c) defines a table to hold the same 24 values. The first column can hold low temperatures, and the second column the high temperatures (or vice versa).

EXAMPLE 5.

The declaration statements below illustrate two ways of defining arrays to hold yearly meteorological data.

```
(a) type
        Data = array [1..365] of Real;
    var
        Lowtemps : Data;
        Hightemps: Data;
        Rainfall : Data;
        Snowfall : Data;
```

```
(b) var
        YearlyData : array [1..365,1..4] of Real;
```

In (a), the array type **Data** is defined, and four one-dimensional arrays of this type are declared. Each will hold daily recordings of specific meteorological data.

The declaration in (b) defines a two-dimensional array with 365 rows and 4 columns to hold the same yearly weather data. Each row will hold one day's readings. The daily low temperatures can be stored in the first column, the high temperatures in the second column, the rainfall amounts in the third, and the snowfall measurement in the fourth.

Since the array has been defined to hold real values, the measurements for temperature, rainfall, and snowfall can all have fractional values.

Access to Array Elements

Any individual element can be accessed from an array by a **subscript** which serves as a pointer into the array to locate the data item desired.

SUBSCRIPT FORMAT

array variable [subscript]
or
array variable [row subscript,column subscript]

array variable is the array whose element is accessed.

[ ] enclose the subscript(s)

subscript is a value in the array's **subscript range** which identifies the element being accessed.

One subscript is required for one-dimensional arrays, while a pair of subscripts to identify the row and column is required for a two-dimensional array.

EXAMPLE 6.

If a year's record of daily weather data has been stored in the arrays declared in Example 5 (a), each day's data can be retrieved by a subscript which identifies that day in the list of 365 values. Thus,

(a) Lowtemps [1]

will access the first element of the array in which the low temperature measured for January 1 is stored.

(b) Hightemps [185]

will access the high temperature recorded for the 185th day, or July 4th in a nonleap year.

EXAMPLE 7.

Assuming the same weather data is stored in the array **YearlyData** defined in Example 6 (b), the readings can be retrieved with the following notation.

(a) YearlyData [10,1]

will retrieve the low temperature for January 10th from the first column.

(b) `YearlyData [185,2]`

will retrieve the high temperature for July 4th from the second column of the array.

(c) Data can be stored in the arrays, or retrieved from them, if the desired date is translated to its corresponding day-of-the-year form to be used as a subscript. Thus, if data for Christmas Day is to be stored, it is necessary to know that December 25th is the 359th day of a nonleap year.

The snowfall amount for Christmas Day can then be stored into

`Snowfall [359] or YearlyData[359,4]`

of the arrays declared in Example 6.

The value of a subscript must be in the range of subscript values declared for the array. If a subscript does not lie in this predefined range, a "subscript out of range" error will occur when the program executes.

EXAMPLE 8.

The array reference

`Rainfall [400]`

will generate an error message since the four meteorological arrays of Example 6 (a) were all declared with the subscript range [1..365].

The subscript of an array reference may be a variable. Its type and value must conform to the subscript range definition of the array.

EXAMPLE 9.

If the program has executed the assignment statement:

`Today   := 91;`

the array reference

`Rainfall [Today]`

will retrieve the rainfall data for April 1st, the 91st day of the year.

Assigning Values to Array Elements

Values can be assigned to any array element with the Pascal assignment operator **:=**   (as described in Chapter 7).

EXAMPLE 10.

The assignment statements:

`Lowtemps [2] := -15.0;`

`Snowfall [2] :=  5.0;`

will store low temperature and snowfall data for January 2nd into the arrays defined in Example 6 (a).

Processing Arrays

When all the elements of an array must be accessed, statements with each individual subscript can be written, as is shown in the next example.

EXAMPLE 11.

The following assignment statements store a student's homework scores into the array defined in Example 3.

```
Homework[1] := 5;
Homework[2] := 7;
Homework[3] := 10;
Homework[4] := 10;
Homework[5] := 8;
Homework[6] := 0;
Homework[7] := 6;
Homework[8] := 10;
```

It is often possible to streamline the processing of a whole array using a variable to which successive subscript values are assigned. This can be done efficiently in a program **loop** where the control variable of the loop serves as an automatically changing subscript. The syntax of Pascal loops is described in Chapter 11.

As is illustrated by the following example, Pascal allows all the values of one array to be copied into a second array in one assignment statement, if both arrays are of the same structure and data type.

EXAMPLE 12.

The assignment statement below copies all 12 values of the array **Mortgage** into the corresponding elements of the array **Rent**.

```
(* Declarations *)

type

    Payments = array [1..12] of Real;

var

    Rent, Mortgage : Payments;

(* Assignment of arrays *)

    Rent := Mortgage;
```

CHARACTER ARRAYS

Strings

.Character data of the type **Char** can be stored in arrays and associated with one variable name, just as numeric values. Such array variables are useful for storing sequences of characters which may represent names, words, or special symbols, usually known as **strings**.

Declaration of Char Arrays

Character arrays must be declared in order to identify a variable name and define the number of bytes reserved to hold its characters.

CHAR ARRAY DECLARATION FORMAT

var identifier : array [1..length] of Char;

var, **array**, **of** are reserved Pascal keywords.

identifier is a name chosen for the array. It must follow the rules for identifiers described in Chapter 7.

: and **[ ]** separate fields of the array definition.

length specifies the number of characters in the array.

Char is the built-in Pascal type for character data.

DEFINITION

(a) Memory is reserved for an array of characters identified by the name given in the declaration.

(b) The number of characters stored in the array is determined by the **length**.

EXAMPLE 13.

The declaration statement below defines a 24-character array named **Title** into which the title of a book can be stored.

```
var Title : array [1..24] of Char;
```

A book title which is stored in the array cannot be longer than 24 characters. A shorter title can be stored in **Title**, but must be **padded** with blank characters at the end to fit the array.

EXAMPLE 14.

The statements below illustrate the alternate method described earlier for declaring array variables:

```
type Name : array [1..12] of Char;
var  LastName, FirstName, MiddleName : Name;
```

The array structure **Name** is defined as an array type, and then used to declare three character arrays. The three variables can store the first, middle, and last name of a person, as long as the names are shorter than 12 characters.

Packed Character Arrays

Because manipulation of character strings is a common operation in programs, Pascal includes a predefined **packed array** type to make string processing more efficient. Memory is conserved in a packed array, because two characters instead of one are stored into one memory word.

The syntax for declaring a **packed array** variable is the same as for a character array, with the addition of the keyword **packed**:

var identifier :   **packed array [1..length] of Char**;

length specifies the number of characters in the array, i.e., the length of the string which the array can hold.

EXAMPLE 15.

The declaration below defines the variable **Line** to be an array capable of holding a line of printer output, typically 80 characters long:

```
var Line: packed array [1..80] of Char;
```

A common technique for programs which use character strings is to define packed array types of predefined lengths, and then declare string variables to be of the appropriate type.

EXAMPLE 16.

```
type
    String2 = packed array [1..2] of Char;
    String4 = packed array [1..4] of Char;
    String10 = packed array [1..10] of Char;
    String16 = packed array [1..16] of Char;
var
    Hours, Minutes, Seconds : String2;
    Year  : String4;
    Month, Day : String10;
    Date, Time : String16;
```

The variables **Hours**, **Minutes**, **Seconds** and **Time** are declared to hold character data representing time, and the **Month**, **Day**, **Year** and **Date** variables will hold data representing a date. Each variable is defined with a packed array length appropriate to hold the string likely to be stored in it.

Accessing Characters

The individual characters of an array of type **Char** can be accessed by a subscript which lies in the interval [1..length] defined in the array's declaration.

EXAMPLE 17.

Given the array declarations of Example 16,

```
Minutes [1]
```

refers to the first character of the **Minutes** array and

```
Date [6]
```

will access the sixth character from the **Date** string.

Assigning Char Values

Single characters may be assigned to individual elements of a character array in a Pascal assignment statement. The values assigned may be constants or variables of type **Char**.

EXAMPLE 18.

```
(* Constant declarations *)
const
    Ampersand = '&';
    Percent = '%';
(* Variable declarations *)
var
    Symbol : Char;
    Password : packed array [1..6] of Char;
(* Assignments *)
begin
    Symbol := '@';
    Password [1] := Ampersand;
    Password [2] := #;
    Password [3] := Symbol;
```

The above statements store the character sequence '&#@' into the first three characters of the 6-character variable **Password**.

Assigning String Values

Strings may be stored in packed character arrays by Pascal assignment statements. Assigned values can be character string literals, or variables and constants declared as packed arrays of the same length.

EXAMPLE 19.

```
(* Array definitions *)
```

```
type
    String6 = packed array [1..6] of Char;
    String8 = packed array [1..8] of Char;
(* Variable declarations *)
var
    City, Capital : String6 ;
    State : String8 ;
(* Constant declarations *)
const
    Hometown = 'Aspen ';
(* Assignments *)
begin
    City := 'Denver';
    State := 'COLORADO';
    Capital := City;
    City := Hometown;
```

The first two assignment statements illustrate the assignment of character string literals to the packed arrays **City** and **State**. The third assignment statement copies a string from one array to another, and the fourth statement stores the constant **Hometown** into a packed array. After the last statement executes, the string 'Aspen' has replaced the string 'Denver' in the array variable **City**.

RECORDS

Record Declaration

An array may be used to hold data in a Pascal program only if all the values to be stored in it are of the same data type. When a collection of data is composed of different types of values, a **record** structure can be defined to hold the data.

RECORD DECLARATION FORMAT

type record type = **record**

    field name : field type;

    . .

        field name : field type
        end;

type, **record**, and **end** are reserved Pascal keywords.

record type is an identifier chosen to name the record structure.

field name is an identifier for a field in the record structure.

field type is the data type of the field.

: must separate the field name and field type.

; must appear as a separator between field definitions and at the end of the declaration.

DEFINITION

(a) A record structure containing the fields listed is defined and associated with the identifier.

(b) Each field has a name and can hold a value of the type specified for it.

(c) Sufficient memory is reserved to hold the fields of the record.

EXAMPLE 20.

The record structure defined below would be appropriate for a used car dealer's inventory program to keep track of the cars on his lot.

```
(* Array declarations *)
type
    String4 = packed array [1..4] of Char;
    Dollars = array [1..3] of Real;
(* Record structure declaration *)
    Car = record
            Make, Model : String4;
            Year : Integer;
            Price : Dollars;
            Class : Char;
            Warranty : Boolean
         end;
(* Variables defined as records of type Car *)
var
    Junker, Deluxe, Sedan : Car;
```

The record structure acts as a template for the information to be stored in the three variables: **Junker**, **Deluxe**, and **Sedan**. Each will hold information about a particular car on the dealer's lot.

An appropriate amount of memory is reserved for each variable to accommodate the types of data values included in the record structure.

Accessing Fields in a Record Structure

Each identifier included in the record declaration is known as a **field**. Data values are stored into fields, just as they are stored into the individual elements of an array.

The value of any field in a record variable is accessed by the following Pascal notation:

variable name.field name

where the name of the record variable and the name of a field are separated by a **.** (period).

EXAMPLE 21.

Given the declarations of Example 20,

```
Sedan.Model
```

will access the model description of a car whose data is stored in the variable named **Sedan**, and

```
Junker.Year
```

will retrieve the model year for a car named **Junker**.

Storing Data into Record Structures

Values can be stored into fields of record variables by assignment statements.

EXAMPLE 22.

The following statements store the information for a new car on the dealer's lot into the **Deluxe** variable:

```
Deluxe.Make := 'BMW ';
Deluxe.Model := '735 ';
Deluxe.Year := 1980;
Deluxe.Price[1] := 4500.00;
Deluxe.Price[2] := 6090.00;
Deluxe.Price[3] := 7499.99;
Deluxe.Class := 'G';
Deluxe.Warranty := True;
```

A record structure may include fields which are arrays, as well as the basic data types. In Example 20, an array of three real values was included in the structure specification. For the **Deluxe** variable of Example 22, the array has been assigned three values which represent the cost of the car to the dealer, the "blue book" value of the car, and the sales price.

The "with" Notation

Pascal provides a shorthand notation for specifying fields of a record. As illustrated below, **with** notation can be used to reference several fields in a record.

EXAMPLE 23.

```
with Sedan do
begin
  Make := 'Olds';
  Model := 'F85 ';
  Year := 1985;
  Class := 'B'
end;
```

*Structured data types allow collections of data to be treated together with one variable name, while allowing individual data elements to be accessed by the use of **subscripts**. Array variables can hold lists or tables of numbers, as well as **strings** of characters. More complex **record** structures can be defined when a collection of data is not all of the same type.*

Array and record variables must be declared in the declaration section of the program in order to reserve memory for the data elements which they will contain. Operations, such as the assignment of values by the assignment operator, can be done on the individual elements of arrays and records. Variable names with subscripts will access individual array elements, and special notation for the field names of a record allow Pascal statements to deal with the individual values of these data structures in the same way as single-valued variables.

9

Arithmetic and Logical Operations

*A*rithmetic computations are an integral part of most computer programs. Pascal includes special symbols for arithmetic operations, and rules which define the order of calulations. Numeric data, represented as variables or constants, can be combined with operators to form complex **expressions** for the calculations of a particular algorithm. The results of computations can be stored into variables, which in turn can be used for further processing by the program.

Logical operations are also an important feature of programs. Comparisons of data and **Boolean** operations allow decisions to be made. Based on the results of logical operations, a program's statements can choose which path of program logic to execute.

ARITHMETIC COMPUTATION

Arithmetic Expressions

Instructions to perform computations in a Pascal program are represented in **arithmetic expressions**. Expressions combine numeric values with **arithmetic operators** to indicate the arithmetic operations which are to be performed. The rules for expressions are described below.

ARITHMETIC EXPRESSION FORMAT

e_1 **operator** e_2

operator is one of the Pascal arithmetic operators defined below.

e_1, e_2 are the operands of the expression. The operands must be numeric constants or variables, or other arithmetic expressions. Arithmetic operations may be performed on either **Integer** or **Real** values according to the rules which are described below.

Arithmetic Operators

Pascal defines the following arithmetic operators:

+ for addition of two values

− for subtraction of two values, and as a **unary** operator to take the negative of a single value

* for multiplication of two values

/ for division of one value by another

EXAMPLE 1.

(a) `14 + 7020`
computes the sum of integer constants 14 and 7020

(b) `-36.5`
represents the negative real value 36.5

(c) `Count + 1`
adds the integer constant 1 to the value stored in the variable **Count**

(d) `Rate * 10.0`
multiplies the value of the variable **Rate** by the real value 10

(e) `Salary / 12.0`
divides the value in the variable **Salary** by the real value 12.

The expression illustrated in (b) is a special case of a simple arithmetic expression where the unary − operator requires only one operand on its right hand side.

Expressions can be far more complex than those of Example 1, and may involve several operators with operands. In addition to simple variables and constants, operands may also be elements of arrays, or fields from record data structures.

EXAMPLE 2.

(a) `b + 5 * Test[2] / 100 - Data`

(b) `Xvalue + Yvalue + Zvalue / XYZ`

(c) `Gross - IncTax - StateTax - FICA + ProfitSharing + Stock.total`

Precedence Rules

When arithmetic expressions are complex, as in Example 2, the intended sequence of operations is not always clear. In Pascal, an implicit sequence is defined for the operations, according to the precedence which has been assigned to all operators.

The precedence of arithmetic operations is defined as follows:

unary –   highest precedence

* and /   next highest

+ and –   lowest

When two operators of the same precedence follow each other in an expression, the computations are performed left to right.

EXAMPLE 3.

According to the rules of precedence, the operations of the expressions in Example 2 will be done in the following sequence:

(a) 5 * Test[2] , then / 100, then + b, then – Data,

(b) Zvalue / XYZ, then + Xvalue, then + Yvalue,

(c) Gross –   IncTax, then – StateTax,   then – FICA, then   + ProfitSharing, then + Stock.total.

Note that **Test[2]** in expression (a) refers to the value stored in the second element of the array **Test**, and the operand **Stock.total** refers to the value stored in the field **total** of a record variable **Stock**.

To force arithmetic operations to be done in a specific sequence, expressions may be enclosed in a set of parentheses, i.e., ( ) symbols. An expression in parentheses will have the highest precedence in a sequence of arithmetic operations. If expressions are nested in a series of parentheses, the sequence of operations will be from the innermost expression in parentheses to the outermost.

EXAMPLE 4.

(a) `((b + (5 * Test[2])) / 100) - Data`

will cause the sequence of operations to be

5 * Test[2], then + b, then / 100 , then – Data

(b) `(Xvalue + Yvalue + Zvalue ) / XYZ`

will cause the sum of the values in Xvalue, Yvalue and Zvalue to be divided by the value in XYZ.

Because of the difference in precedence, the computations of (a) and (b) will produce different results in Example 2 and Example 4.

Data Types of Arithmetic Expressions

The operands of arithmetic expressions may be either **Integer** or **Real** values. However, the data type of the resulting value will depend on the combination of operand types as follows:

Integer + or − or * **Integer** —> **Integer** result

Real + or − or * **Real** —> **Real** result

Integer + or − or * **Real** —> **Real** result

/ —> **Real** result for any combination of operands

INTEGER DIVISION

Because the / operator always computes a **Real** value when the division operation is performed, two special operators, `div` and `mod`, are defined for division of **Integer** values:

a `div` b yields the integral part of the value **a** divided by the value **b**, with any remainder truncated; and

c `mod` d yields the integer remainder of the division of the value **c** by the value **d**.

For the **div** and **mod** operators to operate correctly, the value **b** must not be 0 and the value **d** must be >= 0.

The precedence of the **div** and **mod** operators is the same as for the * and / operators.

Assignment of Arithmetic Results

The results of an arithmetic computation can be assigned to a variable by the assignment operator **:=** . The format of an arithmetic assignment statement is as follows:

variable := arithmetic expression;

EXAMPLE 5.

(a) `A := (b * h) / 2 ;`

will calculate the area of a triangle with base **b** and height **h** into the variable **A**. The operation will yield a Real value and will be successfully executed only if the variable **A** has been declared to be of type Real.

(b) `AvgTemp[5] := (YearlyTemps[5,1] + YearlyTemps`
`[5,2]) / 2;`

will calculate the average temperature for the month of May from the monthly high and low temperatures stored in an array **YearlyTemps**. The result will be stored into the fifth element of another array **AvgTemp**.

(c) `VacationDays := AvailHours div 8;`
   `CarryOver := AvailHours mod 8;`

will compute the number of days available for vacation, and the hours carried over to the next year, for an employee whose vacation time is accumulated by a fixed number of hours each month.

(d) Counter := Counter + 1;

will increment the value in the variable **Counter** by one.

It is important to know that the statement of example 5(d) does not represent an equality of the value on the left of the assignment operator with the value on the right, as it would in a mathematical equation. The Pascal notation **:=** implies an assignment into a memory location. The expression on the right will be computed with the current value of the variable **Counter**, and the result will then be stored into the variable on the left, which in this case is the same variable. When the statement has executed, the value of **Counter** will have been incremented by 1.

EXAMPLE 6.

The arithmetic statements below compute an employee's monthly pay.

```
Bonus := (Salary * SpecialRate) / 12;

MonthlyPay := Salary/12 + Bonus + StockOptions[m] ;

Deductions := (Dependents * Rate) + StateTax + SS + Loan ;

NetPay := MonthlyPay - Deductions;
```

The assignment statements will be executed successfully only if values have been assigned to all variables before these statements are encountered. An error will occur, for instance, if no value has been assigned to the variable **SpecialRate** when the statements are executed.

Although the computation of **NetPay** could have been done in one assignment statement which included all the necessary expressions, the program steps are easier to understand when a complex arithmetic expression is broken down into simpler steps.

Data Types of Assignment Operations

When the arithmetic expression on the right hand side of an assignment statement is evaluated, the data type of the result must be the same as the data type of the variable on the left into which it will be stored. One exception is allowed in Pascal. A computed **Integer** value may be assigned to a **Real** variable, but the integer value will be automatically **converted** to **Real** representation before it is stored.

EXAMPLE 7.

The following statements compute overtime pay from the data stored in the **Hours** array.

```
const
  OvertimeRate = 6.75;
var
  Hours : array [1..5] of Integer;
  Overtime, OvertimePay : Real;
begin
  Overtime := hours[1]+Hours[2]+Hours[3]+Hours[4]
    +Hours[5];
  OvertimePay := Overtime * OvertimeRate;
```

Built-in Functions

The first assignment statement will add together the five Integer values stored in **Hours**, convert the sum to Real format, and store it in **Overtime**. The second assignment statement will multiply the two Real values stored in **Overtime** and **OvertimeRate**, and will store the Real result in the Real variable **OvertimePay**.

Many computations involve the use of special mathematical algorithms which are represented by unique symbols in mathematics. Most computer languages include **built-in functions** which will automatically perform the mathematical calculation when the function name is referenced in an arithmetic expression.

The Pascal notation for a **function reference** is **function (argument)**

where **function** refers to a predefined function name and the **argument** in parentheses represents the data value or expression on which the function's calculations will be performed. An **argument** is also sometimes known as a **parameter** of the function. Each function computes and returns a value of a specific data type. It is also important that the data type of any arguments agree with the data type expected by the function.

The Pascal language includes a number of predefined functions which may be used directly in arithmetic expressions. Some of the most common are

Sqr (x) – Computes the square of a **Real** or **Integer** value x; returns a value of the same type;

Sqrt (x) – Computes the positive square root of a **Real** or **Integer** value x, where x >= 0.0; returns a **Real** value;

Abs (x) – Returns the absolute value of the **Real** or **Integer** argument x;

Sin (x) – Computes the sine of angle x , expressed as a **Real** or **Integer**

value in radians; returns a **Real** value; and

Cos (x) – Computes the cosine of angle x, expressed as a **Real** or **Integer** value in radians; returns a **Real** value.

EXAMPLE 8.

The following examples illustrate the mathematical formulas, and the Pascal equivalents, to compute volume, diagonal and surface area of a cube with a side of length **a**:

(a) $V = a^3$

```
V := a * a* a ;   (* volume of the cube *)
```

(b) $d = a \sqrt{3}$

```
d := a * Sqrt(3); (* length of the diagonal of the cube *)
```

(
c) $A = 6a^2$

```
A := 6 * Sqr(a); (* surface area of the cube *)
```

LOGICAL OPERATIONS

Conditions can be tested in Pascal statements when they are written as expressions whose evaluation results in a Boolean value, True or False. Numeric and character values can be compared by **relational operators**, and more complex logic can expressed by the use of additional **Boolean operators** predefined in Pascal.

Relational Expressions

Two values can be compared in Pascal by writing a **relational expression** as described below.

RELATIONAL EXPRESSION FORMAT

e_1 **operator** e_2

operator is a **relational operator** defined below.

e1, e2 are numeric or character constants and variables, or arithmetic expressions.

Relational Operators. Pascal includes the following **relational operators** for performing comparisons.

=   to determine if two values are equal;

<   to determine if one value is less than another;

<=   to determine if one value is less than or equal to another;

>   to determine if one value is greater than another;

>=   to determine if one value is greater than or equal another; and

<>   to determine if two values are not equal.

The evaluation of a relational expression always produces a **Boolean** result: **True** or **False**.

EXAMPLE 9.

(a) `Result/F > 1250.0`

will determine if the **Real** value in the variable **Result** divided by the value in variable **F** is greater than 1250.0.

(b) `Sum <= Max`

will determine if the value in the variable **Sum** is less than or equal to the value in variable **Max**.

(c) `LastChar <> 'Z'`

will determine whether the character value in the variable **LastChar** is different from the capital letter Z.

(d) `Lotto = '21-7-14-22-5-33'`

will determine if the variable **Lotto** contains the character string expressed between the set of apostrophes.

The operands on both sides of a relational operator must be declared as the same data type. In the case of character strings, both operands must represent a string of the same length, either as a packed array variable or as a character literal.

The result of a relational operation may be assigned directly to a **Boolean** variable in an assignment statement. More commonly, relational expressions are included as tests in Pascal control statements. (Pascal control statements are described in Chapter 11.)

EXAMPLE 10.

The following program segment illustrates the use of relational operators to compute the Boolean values **Test1**, **Test2**, **Test3**, and **Test4**. These values could be used later in **if** statements to make program decisions.

```
(* Constants *)
const
   Result = 1050.0;
   F = 2.5;
   Sum = 65;
   Max = 75;
   LastChar = 'z';
   Lotto = '21-2-14-22-5-33';
(* Logical variables *)
var
```

```
        Test1, Test2, Test3, Test4 : Boolean;
    (* Main program *)
    begin
        Test1 := Result / F > 1250.0;
        Test2 := Sum <= Max;
        Test3 := LastChar <> 'Z';
        Test4 := Lotto = '21-7-14-22-5-33';
```

(a) **Test1** will evaluate to **False**, because 1050.0 / 2.5 is not greater than 1250.0.

(b) **Test2** will evaluate to **True**, because the value 65 stored in the variable **Sum** is less than the value of **Max** which is 75.

(c) **Test3** will evaluate to **True**, because the character z stored in the variable **LastChar** is a different character than the capital Z.

(d) **Test4** will evaluate to **False**, because the character string constant defined as **Lotto** does not match the character string literal in the relational expression.

Note that the = sign is a comparison operator, and the **:=** symbol indicates the assignment of the result to the Boolean variable **Test4**.

Character Comparisons

Two character strings are considered to be equal only if both contain exactly the same sequence of characters.

Other character comparisons are dependent on the relationships assigned to the individual characters of a particular character set. Each character is assigned an **ordinal** number, which defines its place in the sequence of characters.

In the common ASCII character set (defined in Appendix A), the digits '0' to '9' have been assigned ordinal numbers which are less than the capital letters 'A' to 'Z', which are in turn less than the small letters 'a' to 'z'. Therefore, the character 'z' is considered to be greater than the character 'Z', and the character sequence 'MORTON' will be less than the character string 'NORTON', because the character 'N' appears later than 'M' in the sequence of capital letters. That is, the ordinal value of 'M' is less than the ordinal value of 'N'.

Boolean Expressions

In order to allow more complex conditions to be expressed for program decisions, Pascal provides three special **Boolean** operators, which may be combined with relational expressions to form Boolean expressions. The rules for Boolean expressions are described below.

BOOLEAN EXPRESSION FORMAT

b_1 **operator** b_2

operator is one of the three Boolean operators **and, or, not**.

b_1, b_2 are operands with Boolean values. They may be the Boolean constants **True** and **False**, Boolean variables, or relational expressions.

BOOLEAN OPERATIONS

The rules of computation for Boolean operators are defined as follows.

True	and	**True**	—>	True
False	and	**False**	—>	False
True	and	**False**	—>	False
False	and	**True**	—>	False
True	or	**True**	—>	True
True	or	**False**	—>	True
False	or	**True**	—>	True
False	or	**False**	—>	False
	not	**True**	—>	False
	not	**False**	—>	True

As is defined above, the not operator is a unary operator which requires only a single operand on its right.

EXAMPLE 11.

The following examples illustrate the syntax of Boolean expressions in Pascal:

(a) `StopFlag or BreakFlag`

will evaluate to **True** if either of the two variables contains the value **True**, otherwise the result of the operation will yield **False**.

If the two variables have not been defined to be of Boolean type, an error condition will result.

(b) `ValveA and ( XV <= MaxLimit )`

will evaluate to **True** only if the values on both side of the **and** operator are **True**. That is, the value of the variable **ValveA** must be **True**, and the value of the variable **XV** must be less than or equal to the value stored in **MaxLimit**. Otherwise, the result of the Boolean operation will be **False**.

(c) `not ( NextChar = '$' )`

will yield a **True** value whenever the character value in **NextChar** is not the dollar sign. When **NextChar** contains '$', the relational expression in the parentheses will be evaluated to be **True**, and the complete evaluation of the expression will yield a **False**.

Overall Precedence Rules

The expressions of Example 11 illustrate the use of parentheses to control the order of evaluation. Just as with arithmetic operations, Pascal follows implicit rules of precedence with relational and Boolean operations when parentheses are not used.

When arithmetic and logical operations are combined, the order of precedence (highest to lowest) is as follows.

```
( )
- unary minus (with one operand)
not
* , / , div , mod , and
+ , - , or
= , <> , < , > , <= , >=
```

Sequences of operators with the same precedence are evaluated from left to right. Expressions within parentheses are evaluated from the innermost set of parentheses to the outermost.

EXAMPLE 12.

A large company allows an employee to retire with the company's retirement benefits if one of the following conditions is met:

The employee is 65 years old, or

The employee has worked for the company for 30 years, or

The employee is at least 55 years old and has been with the

company for 20 years.

The following Boolean expression will determine if an employee can retire with company benefits.

```
((Age >= 65) or (Service >= 30) or (( Age >= 55) and
(Service >= 20)))
```

The relational expressions in parentheses will be computed first to determine a **True** or **False** values for each subexpression. These values will then be combined with the Boolean operators to determine an overall Boolean value for the expression. Only one of the expressions separated by the **or** operator must be true, for the whole expression to be true. The expression will be evaluated as false if and only if each of the expressions separated by the **or** operator is false.

*A*rithmetic computations in Pascal programs are done in arithmetic statements which evaluate the results of arithmetic expressions and store the computed result into a variable. Arithmetic expressions combine special **operators** and numeric constants and variables to indicate the calculations to be done. Pascal follows an implicit sequence for the operations, unless parentheses are used to alter the order of the computations.

In addition to arithmetic expressions, logical expressions which yield a Boolean result may also be formed with variables and constants. **Relational operators** allow data values to be compared, and special **Boolean operators** allow more complex logical expressions to be evaluated. Boolean expressions which result in **True** or **False** can be used in Pascal control statements as the conditions on which program decisions are based. Program control statements are covered in Chapter 11.

10

Input and Output Operations

*C*omputer programs must be able to read data, and communicate the results of their operations. Many programs interact with their users as they run. Information for the program to use is typed in from a keyboard, and the program's results are displayed on the computer's screen for the user to review. The results may also be sent to a printer so that a report of the program's run can be saved.

When keyboard input is not necessary, input data can be supplied to the program from a file which is stored on the disk. Results can also be stored on the disk for later printing, or for use by another program. Pascal includes statements which control the reading and writing of information, whether it is done via a disk device or directly from the user at the keyboard.

INTERACTIVE INPUT/OUTPUT

System I/O Files

Pascal provides two predefined system files called **Input** and **Output** for reading characters typed in and writing characters out to the screen display or other output devices. Characters are transferred one at a time to these two system I/O files which are known as **text** files. The characters which may be read and written are all those which belong to a computer's base character set, which for most computers is either the ASCII or the EBCDIC character set defined in Appendix A.

127

Read / ReadLn

These Pascal input statements read character data from the system **Input** file, or from other **text** files which are declared in the program (as will be described later).

FORMAT

Read (file name, input list)
ReadLn (file name, input list)

Read, ReadLn are reserved Pascal keywords.

Parentheses must surround the file name and the **input list**.

file name is the name of a previously declared text file. If the file name is omitted, input is read from the system **Input** file.

input list is a list of variables separated by commas. The variables may be of type **Char**, **Integer**, **Real** or **Boolean** and must be previously declared (as described in Chapter 7).

EXECUTION

(a) Characters which represent data items are read from the input file and are assigned to the variables given in the input list. The order of the data items which are entered must correspond to the order of the variables in the list to which they will be assigned.

(b) Numeric and Boolean data items in the input stream must be separated by at least one blank character.

(c) Character data items in the input stream must not be separated by blanks because each blank character is a valid data item.

FILE-POSITION POINTER

A hidden **file-position pointer** always points to the next available character in the file. The **Read** statement advances the pointer to the character immediately after the last character which was read.

END-OF-LINE

The **end-of-line** character is the character transmitted when the **Return** key is depressed on the keyboard. The **ReadLn** statement advances the **file-position pointer** to the next **end-of-line** (EOLN) character in the input stream.

A Boolean system variable called **EOLN** is set to **True** when the **end-of-line** character is read by **ReadLn**.

EXAMPLE 1.

A college admissions office program which processes applications from students might include the following statements.

Note that the <Return> notation indicates that the **Return** key on the keyboard is pressed.

(a) `ReadLn (Gpa);`
will read one data value into the variable **Gpa**.

If the user types

3.45 <Return>

the **Real** value 3.45 (for the student's grade point average) will be stored in the variable **Gpa**, and the file position pointer is advanced to the **end-of-line** character which is entered by the <Return> key. The next input will start on a new line.

(b) `ReadLn (ACT, SATmath, SATverb);`

will read three data values, representing the student's college entrance test scores, into the variables in the list.

If the user types

26 720 650 <Return>

the numeric value 26 will be assigned to the variable **ACT**, the numeric value 720 will be assigned to the variable **SATmath**, the numeric value 650 will be assigned to the variable **SATverb**.

Each data value which is entered must correspond to the type of the variable into which the value is read. Otherwise, an error message will be given. The only exception is an integer numeric value, which may be read into an **Integer** or **Real** variable. Thus the variables **ACT**, **SATmath** and **SATverb** could have been declared as either **Integer** or **Real** variables.

(The declaration of variables is covered in Chapter 7.)

EXAMPLE 2.

Given the declarations

```
var

    Geo: Char;

    Name: packed array [1..20] of Char;

    School: packed array [1..30] of Char;
```

the following statements read the geographic area from which a student applies, the student's name and high school:

(a) `ReadLn (Geo);`

If the user types

`W <Return>`

the letter W would be stored in the **character** variable **Geo**.

(b) `for i := 1 to 20 do Read (Name[i]);`

`ReadLn;`

would read in the characters typed as the name of a student.

If the user types in

Thomas A. Williams   <Return>

the character string 'Thomas A. Williams' will be stored in the array variable **Name**. The spaces before the characters A and W and after the name Williams are typed by pressing the space bar on the keyboard and are stored as the blank character in the array **Name**.

The **ReadLn** statement will read the **end-of-line** character transmitted by the **Return** key and advance the file-position pointer to the beginning of the next line.

(c)
```
k := 1;
while ((not EOLN) and (k <= 30)) do
begin
Read (School[k]);
k := k+1
end;
```

would read the name of the student's high school.

If the user types

Rocky Mountain High School <Return>

the character string 'Rocky Mountain High School' will be stored in the first 26 characters of the variable **School**.

The read process will terminate either when the **end-of-line** character is read, or 30 characters have been read to fill the array, because of the **Boolean** condition which controls the repetition of the statements.

(Pascal statements such as **while,** which control program **loops** such as this one, are described in Chapter 11.)

Since the **Read** and **ReadLn** statements read only one character at a time into a variable of type **Char**, the character strings which represent a student's name and school must be read into the corresponding array variables in a **loop**. Processing of arrays in loops is described in Chapter 11.

Write / WriteLn

These Pascal output statements write characters to the system **Output** file, or to other **text** files which are declared in the program. The system output file is typically the screen of the computer (or possibly a printer).

FORMAT

> **Write (file name, output list)**
> **WriteLn (file name, output list)**

Write, **WriteLn** are reserved Pascal keywords.

Parentheses must surround the file name and the **output list**.

file name is the name of a previously declared text file. If the file name is omitted, output is written to the system **Output** file.

output list is a list of variables, literals, or valid Pascal expressions separated by commas. Variables must be previously declared and may be of type **Char**, **Integer**, **Real** or **Boolean**.

(The rules for using literals and declaring variables are covered in Chapter 7. Rules for writing Pascal expressions are covered in Chapter 9.)

EXECUTION

(a) **Literal** values are written to the output file as they appear in the output list. Character literals are written without the surrounding quote marks.

(b) The values stored in variables of the list are written to the output file.

(c) Values are written in the order in which they appear in the list.

(d) **Real** values are written in **scientific notation** unless a **format** specification is given as part of the variable name.

(e) Expressions in the list are evaluated and their results are written to the output file.

(f) The **WriteLn** command appends an **end-of-line** character after the last character has been written, and any following output will start on a new line.

FORMAT SPECIFICATION

A **format specification** can be added to variables in the list to specify the field width of the output and for **Real** numbers, the number of decimal places to be printed.

The specification is written

variable:w:n

where **w** specifies the field width, and **n** the number of places displayed after the decimal point for **Real** numbers.

EXAMPLE 3.

(a) The statements

```
WriteLn ('Office of Undergraduate Admissions');
WriteLn ('Profile of the Freshman Class:', 1993);
```

would write the following output to the output file:

```
Office of Undergraduate Admissions

Profile of the Freshman Class: 1993
```

The two character strings are written as they appear between the quote marks, and the integer literal 1993 appears as it is written in the output list.

(b) The statements

```
WriteLn;
WriteLn ('Average SAT Scores');

WriteLn;

WriteLn ('College of Engineering', 'Verbal:', EV, ' Math:', EM);
WriteLn ('College of Humanities', 'Verbal:', HV, ' Math:', HM);
```

would write the output:

```
Average SAT Scores

College of Engineering  Verbal: 631 Math: 726

College of Humanities   Verbal: 623 Math: 674
```

if the program had earlier assigned the average SAT score values into the variables **EV, EM, HV,** and **HM.**

The two **WriteLn** statements without an output list will cause a line to be skipped (because an **end-of-line** character will be written).

(c) If a freshman student has been assigned financial aid of $2,500, and the amount is stored in the variable **Aid**, then the statement

```
WriteLn ('Financial Aid = ', Aid);
```

would print

```
Financial Aid = 2.500000E+03
```

because **Real** values are printed in scientific notation.

(d) The statement

```
WriteLn ('Financial Aid =', Aid:8:2);
```

will print

```
Financial Aid = 2500.00
```

because the **format specification** calls for a field width of 8 characters, and 2 decimal places to be displayed for the **Real** value **Aid**.

(e) `Writeln ('College Costs = ', (Total-Aid):10:2);`

will evaluate the **expression** (Total-Aid) in the output list before output is printed.

Prompt Messages

When a program communicates with a user by asking the user to type in values, it is important to give the user a message to indicate when the input data should be entered. Such a message is usually called a **prompt**, and is an output message which must be written immediately before the user supplies the input. The purpose of the prompt message is to serve as a cue for entering data and to inform the user what type of input is expected.

EXAMPLE 4.

(a) The first statement of the pair

```
WriteLn ('Enter Student ID:');

ReadLn ( Id );
```

prompts the user to type in the information which is read into the variable **Id**.

(b) The first two statements of

```
WriteLn ('What type of housing is requested ?');
WriteLn ('Type D for double, S for single:');

ReadLn (Choice);
```

inform the user that the input value to be typed in should be either the character **D** or the character **S**, which then gets read into the student housing choice variable **Choice**.

DISK FILE INPUT / OUTPUT

Input data entered by a program's user, or results created by a program's operations, can be written as output on the computer system's disk storage media for later use. The data is stored in **files** as part of the computer system's **file system** as is described in Chapter 4.

Files

A **file** is a collection of data stored on a computer's disk. These data are a sequence of individual **components** which are all items of the same **type**.

DEFINITION

Data stored in files can be processed by Pascal's read and write statements. All files, except the predefined system I/O files, must be identified in the program by declaration statements.

Text Files. The components of a text file are individual characters which are stored sequentially and are read and written one character at a time, just as the system Input and Output files. A text file may contain end-of-line characters to separate lines of data.

Pascal includes the reserved keyword **text** to declare this type of file.

User-defined files. Disk files can consist of components which are much more complicated than a single character. The components of a file must all be of the same type and each file must be declared to specify what type of data items make up the information in the file.

FORMAT

> **var file name** : **text**
> or
> **type file type** = **file of component type**;
> **var file name** : **file type**

type, **file of**, **text**, and **var** are reserved Pascal keywords.

= and : must be present to separate the fields.

Component type may be any valid data type including Integer, Real, Array, or Record.

file name is the name chosen to identify the file in which information will be stored.

DECLARATION

(a) A file declared as **text** identifies a file with the name **file name** whose components are characters.

(b) The identifier **file type** defines a file whose components have the type **data type**.

(c) A file **file name** is declared whose components are data items of the type **data type**.

EXAMPLE 5.

```
(a) var
       Letter, Memo : text;
```

defines the identifiers **Letter** and **Memo** as text files, which will therefore contain characters as data components.

```
(b) type Students = file of Integer;
    var Enrollment : Students;
```

defines a file **Enrollment** which will be composed of Integer values.

```
(c) type Prices =    record
                        Year : Integer;
                        Low : Real;
                        High : Real;
                        Avg : Real;
                     end;
    type StockPrices = file of Prices;
    var MyStock : Prices;
    Stock   : StockPrices;
```

A variable **MyStock** is declared to be a record consisting of four values, and the file **Stock** is defined to be a file whose components are records of this type.

PREPARING FOR I/O

Before data can be written to a file or read from a file, the file must first be **opened**. That is, it must be located in the file system and prepared for reading or writing. Data may be read from a file or written to a file, but both operations cannot be done on the same file at the same time.

Reset. The **reset** command locates a file in the file system and opens the file for input.

FORMAT

Reset (file name)

Reset is a reserved Pascal keyword.

Parentheses must surround the file name.

file name is the name of a previously declared file.

EXECUTION

The **file-position pointer** is set to the first component of the file so that reading can begin.

EXAMPLE 6.

```
Reset (Enrollment);
```

opens the file **Enrollment** to be read.

Rewrite. The **Rewrite** command prepares a file for output. If the file does not exist, a new file is created. If the file already exists, all previous data in it is cleared.

FORMAT

Rewrite (file name)

Parentheses must surround the file name.

file name is the name of a previously declared file.

EXECUTION

The **file-position pointer** is moved to the beginning of the file so that the first component can be written to the file.

EXAMPLE 7.

```
Reset (Letter);
```

opens the file **Letter** to be read, while

```
Rewrite (Letter);
```

opens the same file for writing, and erases all previous data in the file.

Read

Text files stored on disk can be read by the **Read** and **ReadLn** commands which were described in the first part of this chapter.

Files which have been declared to be of other types can be read by the **Read** command as follows.

FORMAT

Read (file name, input list)

Read is a reserved Pascal keyword.

file name is the name of a previously declared file.

input list is a list of variables separated by commas which are of the same type as the components of the file.

EXECUTION

(a) The first file component is read from the file and is assigned to the first variable in the input list.

(b) The **file-position pointer** is then moved to the next component in the file, which is read and assigned to the next variable in the input list.

(c) This process continues until data has been read into each variable in the list or there are no more data items in the file.

END-OF-FILE

An **end-of-file** character is a special character written after the last component of a file to indicate that no more data follows. A Boolean system variable **EOF** is set to **True** if the end-of-file character has been encountered by a read operation.

EXAMPLE 8.

The statements below will read and display all the student Id's which have been written to the **Enrollment** file, and will also count the number of students:

```
WriteLn ('Enrolled Students');
Count := 0;
while (not EOF) do begin
   Read (Enrollment, Id);
   WriteLn ('Student:', Id);
   Count := Count+1
end;
WriteLn ( Count, 'students enrolled.');
```

Write

The **Write** and **WriteLn** statements can be used to write output to disk files of type **text**, as was described earlier in this chapter.

Data can be written to other types of disk files as follows:

FORMAT

Write (file name, output list)

Write is a reserved Pascal keyword.

Parentheses must surround the **output list**.

file name is a previously declared file which will receive the output.

output list is a list of variables of the same type as the components of the file.

EXECUTION

(a) The data value from the first variable in the output list is written to the output file.

(b) The **file-position pointer** is then moved to point to the next component in the output file and the data value from the next variable in the output list is written to the file.

(c) Any expressions which appear in the list are evaluated and the result is written to the file in the order in which it appears in the list.

(d) The process continues until there are no remaining variables or expressions in the output list.

EXAMPLE 9.

The declaration statements

```
type Percent = file of Real;
var Inflation : Percent;
    InfRate : array [1..12] of Real;
```

define an array called **InfRate** in which the monthly rate of inflation is stored, and a file **Inflation** to which **Real** values can be written.

```
for m := 1 to 12 do
    Write (Inflation, InfRate[m]);
```

will write the 12 monthly values from the array **InfRate** to the output file **Inflation**.

EXAMPLE 10.

Given the declarations of Example 5(c) of a record variable **MyStock**, and a file of **Stock**, the following statements will read in information about a stock and calculate its average price.

```
WriteLn ('Enter year and the low and high stock price:');
ReadLn (Year, MyStock.Low, MyStock.High);
MyStock.Avg := (MyStock.Low + MyStock.High) / 2.0;


If in response to the prompt the user types in
    1990 26.5 82.375 <Return>
```

the year, and the stock's low, high, and average prices can be written to the file as a **record** by the following.

```
Write (Stock, MyStock);
```

*P*ascal input and output statements allow a program to communicate with its user, and to store intermediate data on a computer's disk for later processing.

Dialogue with the user can be handled by the transmission of characters, which are known in Pascal as **text**. Both text and other types of data may be written to data collections known as **files** which are stored in an organized **file system** on the computer's disk. Files must be defined in the program and prepared for reading and writing. **Read** statements are used to read data from files, and **Write** statements will write data to files. The special **ReadLn** and **WriteLn** form of the statments allows data to be processed as lines, separated by a special **end-of-line** character.

11

Program Control

*In some programs, all the operations can be performed by a set of statements which are executed sequentially, one after another. However, when a solution algorithm is more complex, decisions may determine which sections of a program will be executed next. The ability to test a condition and branch to a specific section of code is an important feature of programming languages. Another common technique known as **looping**, allows program statements to be repeated a specified number of times. Loops are efficient methods for processing arrays, for instance, because the value of a subscript can be automatically incremented as a loop is processed.*

*Pascal provides special **conditional** statements for implementing program decisions and loops. There are several modes for writing these statements in order to give the programmer flexibility in directing the computer's operations. The ease of writing control structures in Pascal makes the language especially suitable for writing **structured programs.** As was described in Chapter 5 and 6, well-structured and modular programs are easier to write and to maintain, and are likely to contain fewer errors in program logic.*

SEQUENTIAL PROCESSING

Program body   The section of a Pascal program which contains executable statements is called the **program body** . Statements in the program are processed in sequence, one after another, unless a control type of statement (described below) changes the sequence of operations.

```
begin
    statement;
    statement;
      . .

      . .
    statement;
end.
```

The program body may contain any Pascal statements which are executable. The **begin** keyword must appear at the start of the program body and the **end** keyword, followed by a **.** (period), must be the last statement of the program.

It is common practice to indent the statements between the begin/end pair for better readability.

Compound statements

The **begin/end** keyword pair can be used to define a group of statements as belonging together in a **compound statement**. The compound statement may then be used anywhere in a Pascal program where a single executable statement is allowed.

EXAMPLE 1.

A compound statement to read exam grades and add them to a running total is illustrated.

```
begin
    Student := Student + 1;
    ReadLn (Exam [Student]);
    Total := Total + Exam [Student];
end
```

PROGRAM DECISIONS

When alternative courses of action are needed in a program, a **conditional** statement can be used. In Pascal, the primary conditional statements are the **if** statements. They allow conditions to be tested in order to determine which statements will be executed next.

If/Then statement

This is the simplest form of the **if** statement. It allows a single statement to be executed or skipped, based on the testing of a condition.

FORMAT

if condition **then** statement

if and **then** are reserved Pascal keywords.

condition is a Boolean expression.

statement can be a single or compound statement.

EXECUTION

(a) The Boolean condition is evaluated according to the rules for Boolean expressions defined in Chapter 9.

(b) If the result is **True**, then **statement** is executed. After its execution, program control goes to the next statement in the program.

(c) If the result of the Boolean expression is **False**, the **statement** is skipped, and control goes directly to the next statement in the program.

EXAMPLE 2.

(a) `if Salary <= 44000.00 then Percent:= 7.0 ;`

The variable **Percent** will be assigned the value 7.0 if the value in the variable **Salary** is less than or equal to 44000.00 .

(b) `if (Quiz[j] > 6) then Quizzes:= Quizzes + Quiz[j] ;`

If the value in the jth element of the array **Quiz** is greater than 6, it will be added to the value in the variable **Quizzes**

(c) `if ( Signal and Result <> 0.0) then`

```
begin
  WriteLn ('The result is:', Result );
  Result := 0.0
end;
```

If the Boolean variable **Signal** is **True**, and the value of the variable **Result** is not equal to 0, the value in **Result** will be printed and then set to 0.

If the Boolean condition in parentheses is not True, the compound statement will not be executed.

If/Then/Else statement

This form of the **if** statement allows a choice between two alternative statements to be executed.

FORMAT

if condition **then** statement1 **else** statement2

if, **then**, and **else** are reserved Pascal keywords.

condition is a Boolean expression.

statement1 and **statement2** may be single or compound statements.

EXECUTION

(a) The Boolean condition is evaluated according to the rules for Boolean expressions described in Chapter 9.

(b) If the result is **True**, **statement1** is executed.

(c) If the value of the Boolean expression is **False**, **statement2** is executed.

EXAMPLE 3.

(a) A car rental company charges a fee of $29.95 for daily rentals of its Class B automobiles, or a flat fee of $150.00 for a weekly rental.

A program which computes rental charges might include the following statement.

```
if (Class = 'B' and Contract = 'W') then Charge := 150.00;
                            else Charge := Days * 29.95;
```

(b) A credit card company uses the age of a client to determine credit risk and amount of credit allowed. A credit evaluation program might include the following conditional statement.

```
if (Age < 25) then begin
                CreditRisk := 'H';
                CreditLimit := 500.00
                end
else            begin
                CreditRisk := 'M';
                CreditLimit := Wages * .05
                end;
```

Nested If

If statements may be **nested** by replacing the statement portion of either **if** statement form with another **if** statement. Such nesting allows decisions with multiple alternatives to be expressed in a conditional statement.

EXAMPLE 4.

An insurance company's program may use the following **nested if** statement to choose between one of three possible rates of insurance: a standard rate for the general population, or alternative rates for men and women who are 21 or younger.

```
if Age <= 21 then
   if (Sex = 'M') then Rate := YMrate
               else Rate := YFrate;
          else
          Rate := GPrate;
```

Nested **if** statements can be very difficult to read in a program unless some attention is given to the format in which they are written. Indentation, and the alignment of keywords under each other can make the logic of the statements easier to understand. Although there are no specific rules for indentation, the examples shown here illustrate common formats.

It is also important to make sure that the **nested if** is written correctly so that the alternatives are executed as intended. A decision table or flow chart (as described in Chapter 5) can serve as a useful guide for writing complex conditional statements.

EXAMPLE 5.

A condominium complex in Hawaii gives a discount of 10% to vacationers who stay at least 4 nights in a condo, and 15% to those who stay 7 nights. Owners of condos get a special 30% discount, no matter how many nights they stay. The decision graph of Figure 11.1 showing the various options can aid in writing the nested if statements correctly.

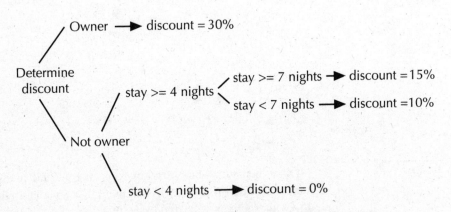

Figure 11.1—Decision graph of rental discounts

The resort's billing program could then include the following statements to determine the discount percentage.

```
(* declarations *)
var
    Owner :  Boolean;
    Discount: Real;
    Nights:  Integer;

begin
   ..

if Owner
then Discount:= 0.3 (* 30% owner discount *)
else if Nights > 4
   then if Nights > 7
      then Discount := 0.15 (* 7 nights discount 15% *)
      else Discount := 0.10 (* 4 nights discount 10% *)
      else Discount := 0.0; (* no discount *)
```

PROGRAM LOOPS

A very useful programming technique is to repeat the execution of a sequence of program statements in a **loop**. Sums and products can be easily calculated with a loop, and it is convenient to process data arrays by iterating a set of statements while changing the value of the subscript of the array.

Pascal contains three options for writing program loops. Each form allows the loop to be controlled in a somewhat different way.

For statement

The **for** statement allows a loop to be set up with a variable which acts as a counter to determine how many times the loop will be executed. This loop form is useful when it is known how many times a set of statements should be executed, and/or when the control variable can be used as a subscript for processing an array.

FORMAT

for variable **:=** initial value **to** final value **do** statement;

for, **to**, and **do** are reserved Pascal keywords.

:= is the assignment operator.

variable is most commonly of type **Integer**, although it may also be a **Boolean** or **Char** type variable.

initial value and **final value** must be constants or variables of the same type as the **variable**.

statement may be a single or compound statement.

EXECUTION

The variable after the **for** is known as the **control variable** for the loop. The single or compound statement which appears after the **do** is known as the **body** of the loop.

(a) When **for** is encountered, the initial value is assigned to the control variable and the body of the loop is executed.

(b) The control variable is incremented to the next value in its sequence. Integer variables are incremented by 1.

(c) The incremented value is compared to the final value. If it is less than or equal to the final value, the statements of the loop are repeated.

(d) If the incremented control value is greater than the final value, no more iterations are made, and the next statement in the program is executed.

EXAMPLE 6.

In mathematics, the **factorial** of a number **n** is defined as:

```
n! = 1 * 2 * . . (n-2) * (n-1) * n .
```

The **for** loop below will calculate the factorial for the value of **Number**:

```
Factorial := 1;
for n := 1 to Number do Factorial := n * Factorial;
```

Note that the variable **Factorial** is initialized to 1 in order to ensure that the computation will begin correctly.

EXAMPLE 7.

A home budget program includes the following statements to calculate the average monthly utility charges for electricity and gas.

```
for Month := 1 to 12 do
  begin
    ReadLn (ElectricBill, GasBill);
    TotalElectric := TotalElectric + ElectricBill;
    TotalGas := TotalGas + GasBill
  end;
  AvgElectric := TotalElectric / 12.0;
  AvgGas := TotalGas / 12.0;
```

The loop reads and computes the totals of 12 monthly electric and gas bills. The average monthly charge is computed after the loop has completed. (Read and write operations are covered in Chapter 10.)

EXAMPLE 8.

For loops are convenient for processing arrays because the control variable can be used as a subscript to access all the elements of the array successively.

If the array **Dow** is used to store daily averages for stock market highs and lows, the loop below can be used to search for the highest and lowest averages that occurred during a year:

```
Low := 9999;
High := 0;
for Day := 1 to 365 do
  begin
    if (Dow[Day] < Low) then Low := Dow[Day];
    if (Dow[Day] > High) then High := Dow[Day]
  end;
WriteLn ('Dow Jones Industrial Average High = ',
High, 'Low = ', Low);
```

The variables which will hold the high and low averages are initialized to constants which will cause the comparisons to start with the first value in the array.

NESTED FOR LOOPS

It is possible to **nest** one **for** loop in another by replacing the loop body of one loop with another **for** loop. This technique is especially useful for controlling subscripts when a two-dimensional array is processed.

In a nested loop, the inner control variable will vary the fastest, and will go through its whole set of iterations for each iteration of the outer loop.

EXAMPLE 9.

A professor uses an array **Exams** to store the scores of the three exams he gives during a semester for the 50 students in his CS120 class. The professor's program uses nested **for** loops to compute exam averages and student scores.

(a) The following statements compute the class average for each of the three exams.

```
for j := 1 to 3 do
begin
  Sum := 0.0;
  for i := 1 to 50 do Sum := Sum + Exams[i,j] ;
  AverageScore:= Sum / 50.0;
  WriteLn ('Average Score for exam ', j, 'was: ', Average
Score:8:2);
end;
```

The row subscript **i** is used to denote the different students, while the column subscript **j** denotes the different exams.

(b) The following statements compute the average score for each student and store the averages in an array called CS120.

```
for Student := 1 to 50 do
  begin
    Sum := 0.0;
    for e := 1 to 3 do Sum := Sum +Exams[Student,e];
    CS120[Student] := Sum / 3.0;
  end;
```

Note, that in each of the two examples above, it is necessary to reset the sum to zero before each new set of additions is started.

While/Do statement

The **while** statement allows a loop to be controlled by a condition which is tested before any of the statements of the body of the loop are executed. The statements in the loop will be executed only if the condition is true.

FORMAT

while condition **do** statement;

while and **do** are reserved Pascal keywords.

condition is a Boolean expression.

statement may be a single or a compound statement.

EXECUTION

(a) The Boolean condition is evaluated according to the rules for Boolean expressions described in Chapter 9.

(b) If the value of the condition is **True**, the statements in the body of the loop are executed.

(c) Control is transferred again to step (a) and the Boolean expression is reevaluated.

(d) If the condition is **False**, the statements in the body of the loop are skipped and control goes to the next statement in the program.

EXAMPLE 10.

An array **Costs** has been set up in a secretary's program to track the cost of office supplies purchased during a month. The array has been allocated 40 values, but it is not predictable how many purchases will be made during the month. The following loop can be used to sum up the purchases and compute the average amount spent on each purchase of office supplies.

```
Supplies := 0.0;
n := 1;
while ( Costs [n] > 0.0 ) do
begin
    Supplies := Supplies + Costs[n];
    Purchases := n;
    n := n + 1;
end;
MonthlyAvg := Supplies / Purchases;
```

It is assumed that the costs of purchases have been stored sequentially in the array, and that the remainder of the array will contain zeroes.

EXAMPLE 11.

A **while** loop is a useful way to control the reading of data, when a predefined value, sometimes known as a **sentinel**, is used to indicate the end of data. In the loop below, no more data is read after the string 9999 is recognized:

```
n := 1;
while ProductNumber <> '9999' do
 begin
   ReadLn ( ProductNumber, Sales );
   Products [n,1] := ProductNumber;
   Products [n,2] := Sales;
   n := n+1
 end;
```

Repeat/Until statement

This form of loop control allows a test to be made after a set of statements has been executed in order to determine whether they should be repeated. Because the test is at the end, the loop will always execute at least once.

FORMAT

repeat statement **until** condition;

repeat and **until** are reserved Pascal keywords.

statement may be a single or compound statement.

condition is a Boolean expression.

EXECUTION

(a) The statement(s) which make up the body of the loop are executed.

(b) The condition represented by the Boolean expression is evaluated according to the rules defined in Chapter 9.

(c) If the condition is **True**, control goes to the program statement which follows the loop and the loop statements are not repeated.

(d) If the condition is **False**, the statements of the loop body are repeated.

EXAMPLE 12.

The following loop will read in student names and assign them to a class until 120 places in the class have been filled.

```
repeat
ReadLn (StudentName);
ClassList[n] := StudentName;
WriteLn (StudentName);
n := n+1;
ClassSize := ClassSize +1;
until ClassSize = 120;
```

The Pascal language provides several types of statements to test conditions which influence the sequence of control through the program. If statements allow alternative statements to be executed, depending on the outcome of a test. The alternatives may be a single statement or a set of executable statements which have been grouped together into a compound statement.

Another useful program control method is the repetition of a group of statements in a program loop. Pascal defines several forms of loops, to allow different ways of controlling the number of iterations. Loops are especially useful for processing arrays, where the loop control variable can effectively be used as a subscript for accessing successive elements of an array.

12

Subprograms

Large *programs are much easier to write when they can be organized into a collection of smaller program modules. Modular programming is the goal of the top-down design techniques discussed in Chapter 5. If the overall programming task is subdivided into smaller tasks, the programmer's attention can be focused on a more limited set of considerations and a better algorithm with fewer errors will be the result.*

Pascal includes definitions for two kinds of subprogram modules. ***Procedures*** *are independent program units whose statements can be activated whenever their operations are needed.* ***Functions*** *have a similar structure, but produce a single result to be included directly in computations. A major advantage of subrograms is their reusability. Once a subprogram has been developed and tested, it can be used again and again in other programs. Some especially useful subprograms, such as routines to sort data or do statistical computations, can be stored in a* ***library*** *of subprograms which can be included in other Pascal programs whenever necessary.*

SUBPROGRAMS

Subprograms are independent sets of statements associated with a name. They are activated by other parts of a program whenever their operations are needed. Control is passed to a subprogram when it is **called** (or invoked), and control is returned when the subprogram's statements finish their execution. Data which must be shared is transferred through an exchange mechanism known as a **parameter list**, which is described later.

All subprograms must be defined in the declaration section of a Pascal program. Once the code for a subprogram is written, it may be invoked as many times as neeeded.

Procedure

A **procedure** is a subprogram module declared as follows.

FORMAT

procedure procedure name (parameter list);
    local declarations
begin
    procedure body
end;

procedure, **begin**, **end** are reserved Pascal keywords.

procedure name is a valid Pascal **identifier** chosen as a name for the procedure.

Parentheses must surround the list of parameters. A procedure may be defined without parameters. If there are no parameters, the parentheses must be omitted.

parameter list is a list of variables representing the inputs which will be passed to the procedure when it is **called**. The rules for specifiying parameters are described below.

local declarations are declarations of variables, constants, and files which are used by the procedure.

procedure body is a single or compound Pascal statement.

DECLARATION

(a) The **procedure** statement is known as a **procedure heading**. It identifies a subprogram with the name **procedure name**.

(b) The variables in the **parameter list** specify what types of values will be available to the procedure when it is called. No values will be passed to the procedure if there are no parameters in the list.

(c) Identifiers declared within the procedure can be used locally by the procedure. They are not defined outside the procedure.

EXECUTION

(a) When the procedure is called, the variables in the parameter list are assigned values by the calling program. No values will be passed to the procedure if there are no parameters in the list.

(b) Control is transferred to the first executable statement of the procedure and the statements of the **procedure body** are executed.

(c) When execution of the procedure statements is completed, control returns to the statement following the procedure call.

PARAMETERS

The parameters in the parameter list of a procedure heading are known as **formal parameters**. They serve as placeholders for the values to be passed to the procedure when it is called.

Parameters in the list must be specified with their type as follows.

FORMAT

(**variable list** : **type**; ... ; **variable list** : **type**)

variable list contains one or more variables of the same type.

type is the Pascal data type of the variables in the list.

; separates variable lists.

, separates the variables in each list.

EXAMPLE 1.

The following procedure compares three Real values, determines which is the largest, and prints a message.

```
(* Procedure to compare three real values *)
procedure Compare (Avalue, Bvalue, Cvalue: Real);
(* temporary variable *)
var Max : Real;
(* procedure body *)
begin
(* determine largest of first two values *)
  if Avalue >= Bvalue then Max := Avalue;
                   else Max := Bvalue;
  (* compare largest of the previous two with the third
*)
  if Cvalue >= Max then Max:= Cvalue;
  (* print results *)
  WriteLn ('Of the three values :', Avalue:6:2,
Bvalue:6:2, Cvalue:6:2);
  WriteLn ('the largest is: 'Max:8:2);
 end;
```

The values to be compared will be passed to the procedure when it is called, and will be substituted for the parameters **Avalue**, **Bvalue**, and

Cvalue. The variable **Max** is a **local variable** which is used by the procedure to store a temporary value.

CALLING A PROCEDURE

A procedure is **invoked** or **called** by writing its name and parameters in the program where its operations are desired. The procedure call may occur anywhere where an executable statement may occur.

FORMAT

pname (parameters)

pname is the name of a previously declared procedure.

parameters is a list of constants, variables, or expressions. The number of values in the list, and the type of each value must correspond to the parameter list defined in the heading of the procedure being called.

EXECUTION

(a) The values in the parameter list are known as **actual parameters**. They are assigned to the **formal parameters** of the called procedure in the order in which they appear in the list.

(b) The statements of the procedure body are executed with substituted values from the calling program's parameters.

(c) When execution of the procedure statements is completed, control returns to the statement following the procedure call.

EXAMPLE 2.

The following program segments illustrate two calls to the **Compare** procedure of Example 1.

(a) If a user at a keyboard types in

             94.60 110.15 102.12 <Return>

in response to the following statements.

```
(* prompt for input *)
Write ('Enter the three readings:');
ReadLn (R1, R2, R3);
(* call the procedure *)
Compare (R1,R2,R3);
WriteLn ('Analysis completed.');
```

The program will print the following.

Of the three values : 94.60 110.15 102.12

the largest is : 110.15

Analysis completed.

The **Compare** subprogram receives the three values typed by the user. They are read into the variables **R1**, **R2**, and **R3** and are passed as actual parameters to the subprogram.

Control is returned to the WriteLn statement for the final printed message after the statements of the **Compare** procedure have executed.

(b) The **Compare** procedure of Example 1 is used to compare values assigned to three Real variables by the following statements.

Function

```
R3:= 2.7;
R4:= 198.20;
R5:= 200.05;
Compare ( 175.55, R5, R3 + R4);
```

will write the following message.

Of the three values : 175.55 200.05 200.90
the largest is : 200.90

In this case, the parameters passed to the procedure for comparison are a constant, one of the previously assigned variables, and an expression involving the other two assigned variables.

A **function** is a named subprogram which computes a value when it is **invoked**. That is, the statements of the function are activated when its name is referenced in an executable statement. The computed result is substituted in place of the function name in the statement which invokes the function.

FORMAT

> **function function name   (parameter list) :   result type;**
>   local declarations
> **begin**
>   function body
> **end;**

function, **begin**, **end** are reserved Pascal keywords.

function name is an identifier chosen as a name to identify the function.

Parentheses must surround the list of parameters. If there are no parameters, the parentheses must be omitted.

parameter list is a list of formal parameters defined according to the rules described earlier for procedure parameters.

result type is the data type of the value computed by the function.

local declarations are declarations of variables, constants, and files which are used by the function.

function body is a single or compound statement. It must include an executable statement which assigns a value to the function name.

DECLARATION

(a) The **function** statement is known as a **function definition**. It identifies a function with the name **function name** whose computations produce a result of **result type**.

(b) The identifiers in the **parameter list** are known as **formal parameters** and specify the input values available to the function when it is called. The parameter list may be empty.

(c) The identifiers declared in the function are known as **local** variables which are defined only during the execution of the function.

EXECUTION

(a) The statements of the function are activated by the appearance of the function name in an executable statement.

(b) The function's formal parameters are assigned values by the calling program. No values will be passed to the function if there are no parameters in the list.

(c) The statements of the function body are executed.

(d) After execution of the function completes, the result assigned to the function name is returned to the calling program. Control returns to the statement which invoked the function.

EXAMPLE 3.

The following statement defines a function and its parameters:

```
function Ratio (Quarter: Integer; Price, Earnings: Real) :Real;
begin
    WriteLn ('Q: ', Quarter, 'P= ', Price, 'E=', Earnings);
    Ratio := Price / Earnings
end;
```

The function's executable statements will compute a Real value into the function name **Ratio**. **Quarter**, **Price**, and **Earnings** are formal parameters which will be replaced with actual values when the function is invoked.

INVOKING A FUNCTION

A function is **invoked** by writing its name and actual parameters in an executable statement where its value is required.

FORMAT

function name (parameters)

function name is the name of a previously declared function.

parameters is a list of constants, variables, or expressions. The number of values in the list and the type of each value must correspond to the parameter list of the function definition.

EXECUTION

(a) The values in the list of parameters are assigned in the order in which they appear to the variables in the formal parameter list of the function which is invoked.

(b) The statements of the function are executed and the computed result is substituted in the expression which invoked the function.

EXAMPLE 4.

The statement below uses the function **Ratio** which was defined in Example 3 to compute the price to earnings ratio of a stock XYZ whose current price is stored in **P** and earnings in **E**.

```
if Ratio (P,E) < 10.0 then WriteLn ('Time to buy XYZ;
P/E < 10');
```

The function is invoked within the conditional part of the **if** statement where the value of the ratio is needed. The 'Time to buy XYZ' message will be printed if the function's computation results in a Real value of less than 10.0.

EXAMPLE 5.

The following program called **Circles** creates a table of 3 columns to store data about 10 circles. The first column contains the radius of a circle, the second column its area, and the third column the circumference. The program includes two functions: one to compute the area of a circle and another to compute its circumference, given a radius **R**.

```
Program Circles;
(* Declarations *)
var
    N : Integer; (* counter *)
    R : Real; (* radius *)
    Data : array [1..10][1..3] of Real; (* table of
values *)
    (* Function to compute the area of a circle *)
    function Area (Radius: Real): Real;

const Pi = 3.14159;
begin
    Area := Pi * Sqr(Radius)
end;
(* Function to compute the circumference of a circle *)
function Circf (Radius: Real): Real;
const Pi = 3.14159;
begin
    Circf := 2.0 * Pi * Radius
end;
begin (* main program *)
(* Loop to read in 10 radius values *)
for N := 1 to 10 do
    begin (* loop body *)
    Write ('Enter the radius of a circle: ');
    ReadLn (R);
    Data [N,1] := R;   (* store radius in column 1 *)
    Data [N,2] := Area (R);  (* store area in column 2 *)
    Data [N,3] := Circf (R)   (* store circumference in
    column 3 *)
    end; (* end of loop *)
end. (* end of program *)
```

The program invokes each function by including its name with the actual parameter **R** directly in the assignment statements which create the table of values. The loop reads in ten radius values which are typed in from the keyboard.

Nested procedures

In Example 5, the functions **Area** and **Circf** are said to be **nested** in the program **Circles**. It is also possible for one procedure or function to be **nested** within another when its declaration appears within another subprogram, as in the following example.

EXAMPLE 6.

In Chapter 4, an algorithm for a program which controls a bank's ATM machine was described. The program which interacts with the user might contain the following procedures.

```
Program ATM;
(* declarations *)
var
  Account : Integer;
  TransType: Char;
  Amount: Real;
(* procedure to process deposit *)
procedure Deposit;
var
  OldBal, NewBal, Dep : Real;
(* nested procedure *)
 procedure Drawer;
 var Lock: Boolean;
 begin
    (* statements to send signal
      to activate drawer *)
 end;
(* body of Deposit procedure *)
begin
    (* statements to add deposit
      to account *)
end;
(* procedure to process withdrawal *)
procedure Withdraw;
var
  Bal, New, Minus : Real;
(* body of Withdraw procedure *)
begin
    (* statements to pass withdrawn
```

```
        amount to user, and update
        account *)
end;
(* main program body *)
begin
    (* statements to determine transaction
    and call correct procedure *)
end. (* end of program *)
```

PROGRAM BLOCK

Example 6 illustrates the definition of procedures within a main program, and the nesting of one procedure within the other.

Each procedure definition is also known as a **block**. A block consists of the declaration part (with parameter list), and the statements which make up the body of the program or procedure.

An **outer block** is a block which contains other blocks, while an **inner block** is one which is inside another block.

In Example 6, the main program ATM, and the procedure **Deposit** are **outer** blocks, while the **Drawer** procedure definition is an **inner** block.

SCOPE OF VARIABLES

When variables are declared in a program or subprogram, their availability for use in different parts of the program is known as their **scope**. In Pascal and other languages there are rules which govern the scope of variables. In Pascal, the scope of a variable is within the **block** in which it is declared.

Global variables. Variables and constants which are declared in a main program are defined for use in the main program and in any of the subprograms declared within the main program. Such variables are known as **global variables** since they may be used anywhere in the program once they have appeared in the declarations of the main program.

In Example 6, the variables **Account**, **TransType**, and **Amount** are global variables which may be referenced in the **Deposit**, **Withdraw**, and **Drawer** subprograms.

Local variables. Variables which are declared within a subprogram are called **local variables** and are available for use only in the **block** in which they have been declared. Variables declared in an **inner block** may only be referenced in the procedure where they are declared. Variables declared in an **outer block** may be referenced in any subprogram which is a part of the block.

Thus, **OldBal**, **NewBal**, and **Dep** are available in the **Deposit** and **Drawer** subprograms, while **Lock** can only be used within **Drawer**. Likewise **Bal**, **New**, and **Minus** only have values in the **Withdraw** procedure.

RECURSIVE PROCEDURES

A subprogram is said to be **recursive** if it can contain a reference to itself as part of its operations. While all programming languages do not allow recursive procedures to be defined, it is a feature of the Pascal language.

Recursive functions and procedures are very useful for certain types of algorithms, and allow streamlined solutions to be programmed. It requires careful analysis of a problem to determine if a recursive solution is possible.

EXAMPLE 7.

The **Fibonacci series** is an interesting mathematical series of numbers, which is related to various natural phenomena. There is even a society whose members study the interesting properties of the Fibonacci numbers.

The first two numbers in the series are 1 and 1, and each subsequent number is defined to be the sum of the previous two numbers. Thus, the first 12 numbers of the series are:

1 1 2 3 5 8 13 21 34 55 89 144 ......

and mathematically, the nth number in the series is defined as:

Fib (n) = Fib (n–1) + Fib (n–2) .

Because the calculation of each Fibonacci number involves the same calculation, i.e., the summation of the two previous numbers in the series, a **recursive** function is an efficient method for calculating a sequence of numbers in the series.

```
(* Fibonacci number calculator *)
function Fib (N : Integer) : Integer;
begin
 if (N = 0) or (N = 1) then Fib := N
          else Fib := Fib(N-1) + Fib(N-2)
end;
```

When the function is called to compute the nth value in the series, it will set the first value to 1, and for every other value will invoke itself, with the previous two numbers in the series as arguments.

Pascal has been designed to keep track of where it was when a recursive function call is made, so that it can back up correctly to the previous step.

The use of subsets of program code which can be invoked as often as needed, is a useful technique for writing efficient programs. Each subprogram can be written to focus on solving a particular part of the solution algorithm. Data which the main program and subprograms need to share can be passed through **parameters***, and the limitations on the scope of declared variables help to reduce unintentional interference between a program's parts.*

Pascal provides two types of subprogram definitions. **Procedures** *are independent routines which can be called whenever their operations are needed.* **Functions** *have the role of computing a single value which can be incorporated directly in an expression in which the function name appears. Pascal also allows* **recursive** *procedures that are able to call themselves in a circular fashion. The capability of incorporating subprograms into a Pascal program helps the programmer achieve the desirable goal of writing well-structured, modular programs.*

Appendix A

The following table shows the binary codes for the ASCII (American Standard Code for Information Interchange) and EBCDIC (Extended Binary Coded Decimal Interchange Code) character sets.

Table A.1

Character	ASCII	EBCDIC
blank	0100000	01000000
!	0100001	
"	0100010	01111111
#	0100011	01111011
$	0100100	01011011
%	0100101	01101100
&	0100110	01010000
`	0100111	01111101
(	0101000	01001101
)	0101001	01011101
*	0101010	01011100
+	0101011	01001110
,	0101100	01001011
–	0101101	01100000
.	0101110	01011100
/	0101111	01100001
0	0110000	10110000
1	0110001	10110001

Character	ASCII	EBCDIC
2	0110010	10110010
3	0110011	10110011
4	0110100	10110100
5	0110101	10110101
6	0110110	10110110
7	0110111	10110111
8	0111000	10111000
9	0111001	10111001
:	0111010	01101010
;	0111011	01011110
<	0111100	01001100
=	0111101	01111110
>	0111110	01101110
?	0111111	01101111
@	1000000	01111100
A	1000001	10000001
B	1000010	10000010
C	1000011	10000011
D	1000100	10000100
E	1000101	10000101
F	1000110	10000110
G	1000111	10000111
H	1001000	10001000
I	1001001	10001001
J	1001010	10010001
K	1001011	10010010
L	1001100	10010011
M	1001101	10010100
N	1001110	10010101
O	1001111	10010110
P	1010000	10010111
Q	1010001	10011000
R	1010010	10011001
S	1010011	10100010
T	1010100	10100011
U	1010101	10100100
V	1010110	10100101
W	1010111	10100110
X	1011000	10100111
Y	1011001	10101000
Z	1011010	10101001

Character	ASCII	EBCDIC
[	1011011	
\	1011100	
]	1011101	
^	1011110	
_	1011111	01101101
`	1100000	
a	1100001	10000001
b	1100010	10000010
c	1100011	10000011
d	1100100	10000100
e	1100101	10000101
f	1100110	10000110
g	1100111	10000111
h	1101000	10001000
i	1101001	10001001
j	1101010	10010001
k	1101011	10010010
l	1101100	10010011
m	1101101	10010100
n	1101110	10010101
o	1101111	10010110
p	1110000	10010111
q	1110001	10011000
r	1110010	10011001
s	1110011	10100010
t	1110100	10100011
u	1110101	10100100
v	1110110	10100101
w	1110111	10100110
x	1111000	10100111
y	1111001	10101000
z	1111010	10101001
{	1111011	
|	1111100	01001111
}	1111101	
~	1111110	

Bibliography

The following books are suggested readings which cover computer science topics and Pascal programming in more detail.

Bach, Maurice J., *The Design of the Unix Operating System*. Englewood Cliffs, N.J.: Prentice-Hall, 1986.

Bierman, Alan W., *Great Ideas in Computer Science—A Gentle Introduction*. Cambridge, Mass.: MIT Press, 1990.

Brookshear, J.G., *Computer Science—An Overview*. Third edition. Redwood City, CA.: The Benjamin/Cummings Publishing Co., 1991.

Capron, H.L., *Computers—Tools for an Information Age*. Second edition. Redwood City, CA.: The Benjamin/Cummings Publishing Co.,1990.

Cooper, D., and M.Clancy, *Oh! Pascal!* Second edition. New York: Norton, 1985.

Dale, Nell, and David Orschalick, *Introduction to Pascal and Structured Design*. Lexington, Mass.: D.C. Heath, 1983.

Dale, Nell, and Susan C. Lilly, *Pascal Plus Data Structures*. Lexington, Mass.: D.C. Heath, 1985.

Goldstine, Herman H., *The Computer—from Pascal to von Neumann*. Princeton, N.J.: Princeton University Press, 1973.

Grogono, Peter, *Programming in Pascal*. Reading, Mass.: Addison-Wesley, 1984.

Janson, Philippe A., *Operating Systems—Structures and Mechanisms*. London: Academic Press, 1985.

Koffman, E.B., *Pascal—Problem Solving and Program Design*. Third edition. Reading, Mass.: Addison-Wesley, 1989.

Pressman, Roger S., *Software Engineering: A Practitioner's Approach*. New York: McGraw-Hill, 1982.

Roberts, Eric S., *Thinking Recursively*. New York: John Wiley & Sons, 1986.

Schach, Stephen R., *Software Engineering*. Homewood, Il.: Irwin, 1990.

Schneider, G.M, S.W. Weingart, and D.M. Perlman, *An Introduction to Programming and Problem Solving with Pascal*. Second edition. New York: John Wiley & Sons, 1982.

Tremblay, J.P., and R.B. Bunt, *An Introduction to Computer Science—An Algorithmic Approach*. New York: McGraw-Hill, 1990.

Index